THE
TALKING LEAVES

An Indian Story

WILLIAM O. STODDARD

1st WORLD
LIBRARY
Literary Society

The Talking Leaves

William O. Stoddard

© 1st World Library, 2007
PO Box 2211
Fairfield, IA 52556
www.1stworldlibrary.com
First Edition

LCCN: 2007934217

Softcover ISBN: 978-1-4218-9688-5
Hardcover ISBN: 978-1-4218-9788-2
eBook ISBN: 978-1-4218-9588-8

Purchase *"The Talking Leaves"*
as a traditional bound book at:
www.1stWorldLibrary.com/purchase.asp?ISBN=978-1-4218-9688-5

1st World Library is a literary, educational organization
dedicated to:

- Creating a free internet library of downloadable ebooks

- Hosting writing competitions and offering book publishing
scholarships.

Interested in more 1st World Library books? contact:
literacy@1stworldlibrary.com
Check us out at: www.1stworldlibrary.com

1ˢᵗ World Library Literary Society

Giving Back to the World

"If you want to work on the core problem, it's early school literacy."

- James Barksdale, former CEO of Netscape

"No skill is more crucial to the future of a child, or to a democratic and prosperous society, than literacy."

- Los Angeles Times

"Literacy... means far more than learning how to read and write... The aim is to transmit... knowledge and promote social participation."

- UNESCO

"Literacy is not a luxury, it is a right and a responsibility. If our world is to meet the challenges of the twenty-first century we must harness the energy and creativity of all our citizens."

- President Bill Clinton

"Parents should be encouraged to read to their children, and teachers should be equipped with all available techniques for teaching literacy, so the varying needs and capacities of individual kids can be taken into account."

- Hugh Mackay

CHAPTER I

"Look, Rita! look!"

"What can it mean, Ni-ha-be?"

"See them all get down and walk about."

"They have found something in the grass."

"And they're hunting for more."

Rita leaned forward till her long hair fell upon the neck of the beautiful little horse she was riding, and looked with all her eyes.

"Hark! they are shouting."

"You could not hear them if they did."

"They look as if they were."

Ni-ha-be sat perfectly still in her silver-mounted saddle, although her spirited mustang pony pawed the ground and pulled on his bit as if he were in a special hurry to go on down the side of the mountain.

The two girls were of about the same size, and could not either of them have been over fifteen years old. They were both very pretty, very well dressed and well mounted, and they could both speak in a strange, rough, and yet musical language; but there was no other resemblance between them.

"Father is there, Rita."

"Can you see him?"

"Yes, and so is Red Wolf."

"Your eyes are wonderful. Everybody says they are."

Ni-ha-be might well be proud of her coal-black eyes, and of the fact that she could see so far and so well with them. It was not easy to say just how far away was that excited crowd of men down there in the valley. The air was so clear, and the light so brilliant among those snow-capped mountain ranges, that even things far off seemed sometimes close at hand.

For all that there were not many pairs of eyes, certainly not many brown ones like Rita's, which could have looked, as Ni-ha-be did, from the pass into the faces of her father and brother and recognized them at such a distance.

She need not have looked very closely to be sure of one thing more—there was not a single white man to be seen in all that long, deep, winding green valley.

Were there any white women?

There were plenty of squaws, old and young, but not one woman with a bonnet, shawl, parasol, or even so much as a pair of gloves. Therefore, none of them could have been white.

William O. Stoddard

Rita was as well dressed as Ni-ha-be, and her wavy masses of brown hair were tied up in the same way, with bands of braided deer-skin, but neither of them had ever seen a bonnet. Their sunburnt, healthy faces told that no parasol had ever protected their complexions, but Ni-ha-be was a good many shades the darker. There must have been an immense amount of hard work expended in making the graceful garments they both wore. All were of fine antelope-skin; soft, velvety, fringed, and worked and embroidered with porcupine quills. Frocks and capes and leggings and neatly fitting moccasins, all of the best, for Ni-ha-be was the only daughter of a great Apache chief, and Rita was every bit as important a person according to Indian notions, for Ni-ha-be's father had adopted her as his own.

Either one of them would have been worth a whole drove of ponies or a wagon-load of guns and blankets, and the wonder was that they had been permitted to loiter so far behind their friends on a march through that wild, strange, magnificent land.

Had they been farther to the east, or south, or north, it is likely they would have been kept with the rest pretty carefully; but Many Bears and his band were on their way home from a long buffalo-hunt, and were already, as they thought, safe in the Apache country—away beyond any peril from other tribes of Indians, or from the approach of the hated and dreaded white men.

To be sure, there were grizzly bears and wolves and other wild animals to be found among those mountain passes, but they were not likely to remain very near a band of hunters like the one now gathered in that valley.

Great hunters, brave warriors, well able to take care of themselves and their families, but just now they were very much excited about something—something on the ground.

The younger braves, to the number of more than a hundred, were standing back respectfully, while the older and more experienced warriors carefully examined a number of deep marks on the grass around a bubbling spring.

There had been a camp there not long before, and the first discovery made by the foremost Apache who had ridden up to that spring was that it had not been a camp of his own people.

The prints of the hoofs of horses showed that they had been shod, and there are neither horseshoes nor blacksmiths among the red men of the South-west.

The tracks left by the feet of men were not such as can be made by moccasins. There are no heels on moccasins, and no nails in the soles of them.

Even if there had been Indian feet in the boots, the toes would not have been turned out in walking. Only white men do that.

So much was plain at a mere glance; but there were a good many other things to be studied and interpreted before Many Bears and his followers could feel satisfied.

It was a good deal like reading a newspaper. Nobody tears one up till it has been read through, and the Apaches did not trample the ground around the spring till they had searched out all that the other tramplings could tell them.

Then the dark-faced, ferocious looking warriors who had made the search all gathered around their chief and, one after another, reported what they had found.

William O. Stoddard

There had been a strong party of white men at that spot three days before; three wagons, drawn by mule teams; many spare mules; twenty-five men who rode horses, besides the men who drove the wagons.

"Were they miners?"

Every warrior and chief was ready to say "No" at once.

"Traders?"

No, it could not have been a trading-party.

"All right," said Many Bears, with a solemn shake of his gray head. "Blue-coats—cavalry. Come from Great Father at Washington—no stay in Apache country—go right through —not come back—let them go."

Indian sagacity had hit the nail exactly on the head; for that had been a camp of a United States military exploring expedition, looking for passes and roads, and with instructions to be as friendly as possible with any wandering red men they might meet.

Nothing could be gained by following such a party as that, and Many Bears and his band began at once to arrange their own camp, for their morning's march through the pass had been a long and fatiguing one.

If the Apache chief had known a very little more, he would have sent his best scouts back upon the trail that squad of cavalry had come by, till he found out whether all who were travelling by that road had followed it as far as the spring. He might thus have learned something of special importance to him. Then, at the same time, he would have sent other scouts back upon his own trail, to see if anybody was following him, and what for. He might have learned a good deal more important news in that way.

He did nothing of the kind; and so a very singular discovery was left for Rita and Ni-ha-be to make, without any help at all.

As they rode out from the narrow pass, down the mountain-side, and came into the valley, it was the most natural thing in the world for them to start their swift mustangs on a free gallop; not directly toward the camping-place, for they knew well enough that no girls of any age would be permitted to approach very near to warriors gathered in council. Away to the right they rode, following the irregular curve of the valley, side by side, managing the fleet animals under them as if horse and rider were one person.

So it came to pass that before the warriors had completed their task the two girls had struck the trail along which the blue-coated cavalry had entered the valley.

"Rita, I see something."

"What is it?"

"Come! See! Away yonder."

Rita's eyes were as good as anybody's, always excepting Apaches' and eagles', and she could see the white fluttering object at which her adopted sister was pointing.

The marks of the wheels and all the other signs of that trail, as they rode along, were quite enough to excite a pair of young ladies who had never seen a road, a pavement, a sidewalk, or anything of the sort; but when they came to that white thing fluttering at the foot of a mesquite-bush they

William O. Stoddard

both sprung from their saddles at the same instant.

One, two, three—a good deal dog's-eared and thumb-worn, for they had been read by every man of the white party who cared to read them before they were thrown away, but they were very wonderful yet. Nothing of the kind had ever before been imported into that region of the country.

Ni-ha-be's keen black eyes searched them in vain, one after another, for anything she had ever seen before.

"Rita, you are born white. What are they?"

Poor Rita!

Millions and millions of girls have been "born white," and lived and died with whiter faces than her own rosy but sun-browned beauty could boast, and yet never looked into the fascinating pages of an illustrated magazine.

How could any human being have cast away in the wilderness such a treasure?

Rita was sitting on the grass, with one of the strange prizes open in her lap, rapidly turning the leaves, and more excited by what she saw than were Many Bears and his braves by all they were discovering upon the trampled level around the spring.

"Rita," again exclaimed Ni-ha-be, "what are they?"

"They are talking leaves," said Rita.

CHAPTER II

"Did you say, Murray, there were any higher mountains than these?"

"Higher'n these? Why, Steve, the mountains we crossed away back there, just this side of the Texas border, were twice as high, some of them."

"These are big enough. Are there any higher mountains in the world than ours? Did you ever see any?"

"I've seen some of them. I've heard it said the tallest are in India. South America can beat us. I've seen the Andes."

"I don't want to see anything that looks worse to climb than this range right ahead of us."

"Where the Apaches got through, Steve, we can. They're only a hunting-party, too."

"More warriors than we have."

"Only Apaches, Steve. Ours are Lipans. There's a big difference in that, I tell you."

"The Lipans are your friends."

"Yours too, and you must let them think you are their friend—strong. The Apaches are everybody's enemies—mine, yours—only fit to be killed off."

"You've killed some of 'em."

"Not so many as I mean to kill. That's one thing I'm on this trip for. Old Two Knives would almost have given it up if it hadn't been for me."

"I don't feel that way about the Lipans if they did capture me. All I want of them is to get away and go back to the settlements."

"Maybe your folks won't know you when you come."

Steve looked down at his fine muscular form from limb to limb, while the stern, wrinkled face of his companion almost put on a smile.

"I'd have to wash, that's a fact."

"Get off your war-paint. Put on some white men's clothing. Cut your hair."

"They'd know me then."

"You've grown a head taller since you was captured, and they've made a Lipan of you all over but in two places."

"What are they?"

"Your eyes and hair. They're as light as mine were when I was of your age."

"I'm not a Lipan inside, Murray, nor any other kind of

Indian. It would take more than three years to do that."

"I've been among 'em seven. But then I never would paint."

The sun and the wind had painted him darkly enough; and if his hair had once been "light," it was now as white as the tops of the mountains he and Steve had been looking at.

Behind them, on a barren sandy level, through which ran a narrow stream of ice-cold water, about three-score of wild-looking human beings were dismounted, almost in a circle, each holding the end of a long "lariat" of strong hide, at the other end of which was a horse.

Some seemed to have two and even three horses, as if they were on an errand which might use up one and call for another. That was quite likely, for Lipan warriors are terribly hard riders.

Those who had now but one horse had probably worn out their first mount and turned him adrift by the way-side, to be picked up, Indian fashion, on the way home.

When a plains Indian leaves a horse in that way, and does not find him again, he tries his best to find some other man's horse to take his place.

More than sixty Indian warriors, all in their war-paint, armed to the teeth, with knives, revolvers, repeating-rifles of the best and latest patterns, and each carrying a long steel-headed Mexican lance.

Not a bow or arrow or war-club among them. All such weapons belong to the old, old times, or to poor, miserable, second-rate Indians, who cannot buy anything better. The fierce and haughty Lipans and Comanches, and other warlike tribes, insist on being armed as well as the United States troops, and even better.

What could a cavalryman do with a lance?

About as much as an Indian with a sword; for that is one weapon the red men could never learn the use of, from King Philip's day to this.

It was luncheon-time with that Lipan war-party, and they were hard at work on their supplies of dried venison and cold roast buffalo-meat.

Their halt would not be a long one in a spot where there was no grass for their horses, but they could hold a council while they were eating, and they could listen to a speech from the short, broad, ugly-looking old chief who now stood in the middle of the circle.

"To-la-go-to-de will not go back now till he has struck the Apaches. He has come too far. The squaws of his village would laugh at him if he rode through the mountains and came back to them with empty hands."

That was the substance of his address, put again and again in different shapes, and it seemed to meet the approval of his listeners.

There is nothing a Lipan brave is really afraid of except ridicule, and the dread of being laughed at was the strongest argument their leader could have used to spur them forward.

Once, indeed, he made another sharp hit by pointing to the spot where Murray and Steve were standing.

"No Tongue has the heart of a Lipan. He says if we go back

he will go on alone. He will take the Yellow Head with him. They will not be laughed at when they come back. Will the Lipans let their squaws tell them they are cowards, and dare not follow an old pale-face and a boy?"

A deep, half-angry "ugh" went around the circle.

To-la-go-to-de had won over all the grumblers in his audience, and need not have talked any more.

He might have stopped right there and proceeded to eat another slice of buffalo-meat, but when an Indian once learns to be an orator he would rather talk than eat, any day.

In fact, they are such talkers at home and among themselves, that Murray had earned the queer name given him by the chief in no other way than by his habitual silence. He rarely spoke to anybody, and so he was "No Tongue."

The chief himself had a name of which he was enormously proud, for he had won it on a battle-field. His horse had been killed under him, in a battle with the Comanches, when he was yet a young warrior, and he had fought on foot with a knife in each hand.

From that day forward he was To-la-go-to-de, or "The chief that fights with two knives."

Any name he may have been known by before that was at once dropped and forgotten.

It is a noteworthy custom, but the English have something almost exactly like it. A man in England may be plain Mr. Smith or Mr. Disraeli for ever so many years, and then all of a sudden he becomes Lord So-and-So, and nobody ever speaks of him again by the name he carried when he was a mere "young brave."

It is a great mistake to suppose the red men are altogether different from the white.

As for Steve, his hair was nearer chestnut than yellow, but it had given him his Indian name; one that would stick to him until, like To-la-go-to-de, he should distinguish himself in battle and win a "war name" of his own.

He and Murray, however they might be regarded as members of the tribe and of that war-party, had no rights in the "Council." Only born Lipans could take part in that, except by special invitation.

It happened, on the present occasion, that they were both glad of it, for No Tongue had more than usual to say, and Yellow Head was very anxious to listen to him.

"That peak yonder would be an awful climb, Steve."

"I should say it would."

"But if you and I were up there, I'll tell you what we could do; we could look north and east into New Mexico, north and west into Arizona, and south every way, into Mexico itself."

"Are we so near the border?"

"I think we are."

Something like a thunder-cloud seemed to be gathering on Murray's face, and the deep furrows grew deeper, in great rigid lines and curves, while his steel-blue eyes lighted up with a fire that made them unpleasant to look upon.

"You lived in Mexico once?"

"Did I? Did I ever tell you that?"

"Not exactly. I only guessed it from things you've dropped."

"I'll tell you now, then. I did live in Mexico—down yonder in Chihuahua."

"She-waw-waw?" said Steve, trying to follow the old man's rapid pronunciation of the strange, musical name.

"Down there, more than a hundred miles south of the border. I thought we were safe. The mine was a good one. The hacienda was the prettiest place I could make of it. I thought I should never leave it. But the Apaches came one day—"

He stopped a moment and seemed to be looking at the tops of the western mountains.

"Did you have a fight with them?" asked Steve.

"Fight? No. I was on a hunt in the sierras that day. When I came home it was all gone."

"The Apaches?"

"The mine was there, but the works were all burnt. So was the hacienda and the huts of the peons and workmen. Everything that would burn."

"But the people!"

"Cattle, horses, all they could drive with them, they carried away. We won't say anything about the people, Steve. My wife was among them. She was a Spanish-Mexican lady. She

William O. Stoddard

owned the mine and the land. We buried her before we set out after the Apaches. I've been following them ever since."

"Were the rest all killed?"

"All. They did not even leave me my little girl. I hadn't anything left to keep me there."

"So you joined the Lipans?"

"They're always at war with the Apaches. I'm pretty near to being an Indian now."

"I won't be, then. I'll get away, somehow. I'm white, and I'm almost a man."

"Steve, have you forgotten anything you knew the day they took you prisoner?"

"No, I haven't. I was fifteen then, and if there's one thing I've been afraid of it was that I would forget. I've repeated things over and over and over, for fear they'd get away from me."

"That's all right. I've had an eye on you about that. But haven't you learned something?"

"You've taught me all about rocks and stones and ores and mining—"

"Yes, and you can ride like a Lipan, and shoot and hunt, and there isn't a young brave in the band that can throw you in a fair wrestle."

"That's all Indian—"

"Is it? Well, whether it is or not, you'll need it all before long. All you know."

"To fight Apaches?"

"Better'n that, Steve. It's been of no use for you to try to get away toward Texas. They watch you too closely, and besides, the Comanches are most of the time between us and the settlements. They won't watch you at all out here. That's why I insisted on bringing you along."

"Do you mean I'll have a chance to get away?"

"I don't mean you shall go back of the mountains again, Steve. You must wait patiently, but the time'll come. I tell you what, my boy, when you find yourself crossing the Arizona deserts and mountains all alone, you'll be right glad you can ride, and shoot, and hunt, and find your own way. It's all Indian knowledge, but it's wonderfully useful when you have to take care of yourself in an Indian country."

The dark cloud was very heavy on Murray's face yet, but an eager light was shining upon that of his young friend—the light of hope.

William O. Stoddard

CHAPTER III

"Talking leaves?" said Ni-ha-be, as she turned over another page of the pamphlet in her lap and stared at the illustrations. "Can you hear what they say?"

"With my eyes."

"Then they are better than mine. I am an Apache! You was born white!"

There was a little bit of a flash in the black eyes of the Indian maiden. She had not the least idea but that it was the finest thing in all the world to be the daughter of Many Bears, the great Apache warrior, and it did not please her to find a mere white girl, only Indian by adoption, able to see or hear more than she could.

Rita did not reply for a moment, and a strange sort of paleness crept across her face, until Ni-ha-be exclaimed,

"It hurts you, Rita! It is bad medicine. Throw it away."

"No, it does not hurt—"

"It makes you sick?"

"No, not sick—it says too much. It will take many days to hear it all."

"Does it speak Apache?"

"No. Not a word."

"Nor the tongue of the Mexican pony men?"

"No. All it says is in the tongue of the blue-coated white men of the North."

"Ugh!"

Even Ni-ha-be's pretty face could express the hatred felt by her people for the only race of men they were at all afraid of.

There were many braves in her father's band who had learned to talk Mexican-Spanish. She herself could do so very well, but neither she nor any of her friends or relatives could speak more than a few words of broken English, and she had never heard Rita use one.

"There are many pictures."

"Ugh! yes. That's a mountain, like those up yonder. There are lodges, too, in the valley. But nobody ever made lodges in such a shape as that."

"Yes, or nobody could have painted a talking picture of them."

"It tells a lie, Rita! And nobody ever saw a bear like that."

"It isn't a bear, Ni-ha-be. The talking leaf says it's a lion."

"What's that? A white man's bear?"

Rita knew no more about lions than did her adopted sister, but by the time they had turned over a few more pages their curiosity was aroused to a high degree. Even Ni-ha-be wanted to hear all that the "talking leaves" might have to say in explanation of those wonderful pictures.

It was too bad of Rita to have been "born white" and not to be able to explain the work of her own people at sight.

"What shall we do with them, Ni-ha-be?"

"Show them to father."

"Why not ask Red Wolf?"

"He would take them away and burn them. He hates the pale-faces more and more every day."

"I don't believe he hates me."

"Of course not. You're an Apache now. Just as much as Mother Dolores, and she's forgotten that she was ever white."

"She isn't very white, Ni-ha-be. She's darker than almost any other woman in the tribe."

"We won't show her the talking leaves till father says we may keep them. Then she'll be afraid to touch them. She hates me."

"No, she doesn't. She likes me best, that's all."

"She'd better not hate me, Rita. I'll have her beaten if she isn't good to me. I'm an Apache!"

The black-eyed daughter of the great chief had plenty of self-will and temper. There could be no doubt of that. She sprang upon her mustang with a quick, impatient bound, and Rita followed, clinging to her prizes, wondering what would be the decision of Many Bears and his councillors as to the ownership of them.

A few minutes of swift riding brought the two girls to the border of the camp.

"Rita? Red Wolf!"

"I see him—he is coming to meet us, but he does not want us to think so."

That was a correct guess.

The tall, hawk-nosed young warrior, who was now riding toward them, was a perfect embodiment of Indian haughtiness, and even his sister was a mere "squaw" in his eyes. As for Rita, she was not only a squaw but also not even a full-blooded Apache, and was to be looked down upon accordingly.

He was an Indian and a warrior, and would one day be a chief like his father.

Still, he had so far unbent his usual cold dignity as to turn his horse to meet that sisterly pair, if only to find out why they were in such a hurry.

"What scare you?"

"We're not scared. We've found something—pale-face sign."

"Apache warriors do not ask squaws if there are pale-faces near them. The chiefs know all; their camp was by the spring."

"Was it?" exclaimed Ni-ha-be. "We have found some of their talking leaves. Rita must show them to father."

"Show them to me!"

"No. You are an Apache; you cannot hear what they say: Rita can—she is white."

"Ugh! Show leaves, now!"

Ni-ha-be was a "squaw," but she was also something of a spoiled child, and was less afraid of her brother than he may have imagined. Besides, the well-known rule of the camp, or of any Indian camp, was in her favor.

All "signs" were to be reported to the chief by the finder, and Ni-ha-be would make her report to her father like a warrior.

Rita was wise enough to say nothing, and Red Wolf was compelled to soften his tone a little. He even led the way to the spot near the spring where the squaws of Many Bears were already putting up his "lodge."

There was plenty of grass and water in that valley, and it had been decided to rest the horses there for three days, before pushing on deeper into the Apache country.

The proud old chief was not lowering his dignity to any such work as lodge-pitching. He would have slept on the bare ground without a blanket before he would have touched one pole with a finger.

That was "work for squaws," and all that could be expected of him was that he should stand near and say "Ugh!" pleasantly, when things were going to please him, and to say it in a different tone if they were not.

Ni-ha-be and Rita were favorites of the scarred and wrinkled warrior, however, and when they rode up with Red Wolf, and the latter briefly stated the facts of the case—all he knew of them—the face of Many Bears relaxed into a grim smile.

"Squaw find sign. Ugh! Good!"

"Rita says they are talking leaves. Much picture. Many words. See!"

Her father took from Ni-ha-be, and then from Rita, the strange objects they held out so excitedly, but to their surprise he did not seem to share in their estimate of them.

"No good. See them before. No tell anything true. Big lie."

Many Bears had been among the forts and border settlements of the white men in his day. He had talked with army officers and missionaries and government agents. He had seen many written papers and printed papers, and had had books given him, and there was no more to be told or taught him about nonsense of that kind. He had once imitated a pale-faced friend of his, and looked steadily at a newspaper for an hour at a time, and it had not spoken a word to him.

So now he turned over the three magazines in his hard, brown hand, with a look of dull curiosity mixed with a good deal of contempt.

"Ugh! Young squaws keep them. No good for warriors. Bad medicine. Ugh!"

William O. Stoddard

Down they went upon the grass, and Rita was free to pick up her despised treasures and do with them as she would. As for Red Wolf, after such a decision by his terrible father, he would have deemed it beneath him to pay any farther attention to the "pale-face signs" brought into camp by two young squaws.

Another lodge of poles and skins had been pitched at the same time with that of Many Bears, and not a great distance from it. In fact, this also was his own property, although it was to cover the heads of only a part of his family.

In front of the loose "flap" opening, which served for the door of this lodge, stood a stout, middle-aged woman, who seemed to be waiting for Ni-ha-be and Rita to approach. She had witnessed their conference with Many Bears, and she knew by the merry laugh with which they gathered up their fallen prizes that all was well between them and their father. All the more for that, it may be, her mind was exercised as to what they had brought home with them which should have needed the chief's inspection.

"Rita!"

"What, Ni-ha-be?"

"Don't tell Mother Dolores a word. See if she can hear for herself."

"The leaves won't talk to her. She's Mexican white, not white from the North."

Nobody would have said to look at her, that the fat, surly-faced squaw of Many Bears was a white woman of any sort. Her eyes were as black and her long, jetty hair was as thick and coarse, and her skin was every shade as dark as were those of any Apache house-keeper among the scattered lodges of that hunting-party.

She was not the mother of Ni-ha-be. She had not a drop of Apache blood in her veins, although she was one of the half-dozen squaws of Many Bears. Mother Dolores was a pure "Mexican," and therefore as much of an Indian, really, as any Apache, or Lipan, or Comanche. Only a different kind of an Indian, that was all.

Her greeting to her two young charges, for such they were, was somewhat gruff and brief, and there was nothing very respectful in the manner of their reply. An elderly squaw, even though the wife of a chief, is never considered as anything better than a sort of servant, to be valued according to the kind and quantity of the work she can do. Dolores could do a great deal, and was therefore more than usually respectable; and she had quite enough force of will to preserve her authority over two such half-wild creatures as Ni-ha-be and Rita.

"You are late. Come in! Tell me what it is!"

Rita was as eager now as Ni-ha-be had been with her father and Red Wolf; but even while she was talking Dolores pulled them both into the lodge.

"Talking leaves!"

Not Many Bears himself could have treated those poor magazines with greater contempt than did the portly dame from Mexico. To be sure, it was many a long year since she had been taken a prisoner and brought across the Mexican border, and reading had not been among the things she had learned before coming.

"Rita can tell us all they say, by-and-by, Mother Dolores."

"Let her, then. Ugh!"

She turned page after page, in a doubtful way, as if it were quite possible one of them might bite her, but suddenly her whole manner changed.

"Ugh!"

"Rita," exclaimed Ni-ha-be, "the leaves have spoken to her."

She had certainly kissed one of them. Then she made a quick motion with one hand across her brow and breast.

"Give it to me, Rita! You must give it to me!"

Rita held out her hand for the book, and both the girls leaned forward with open mouths to learn what could have so disturbed the mind of Dolores.

It was a picture.

A sort of richly carved and ornamented door-way, but with no house behind it, and in it a lady with a baby in her arms, and over it a great cross of stone.

"Yes, Dolores," said Rita, "we will give you that leaf."

It was quickly cut out, and the two girls wondered more and more to see how the fingers of Dolores trembled as they closed upon that bit of paper.

She looked at the picture again with increasing earnestness. Her lips moved silently, as if trying to utter words her mind had lost.

Then her great fiery black eyes slowly closed, and the amazement of Ni-ha-be and Rita was greater than they could have expressed, for Mother Dolores sunk upon her knees hugging that picture. She had been an Apache Indian for long years, and was thoroughly "Indianized," but upon that page had been printed a very beautiful representation of a Spanish "Way-side Shrine of the Virgin."

William O. Stoddard

CHAPTER IV

A mountain range is not at all like a garden fence. You do not just climb up one side of it and drop down into another garden beyond.

The one which arose before the Lipans that day, and through which the Apaches before them had driven their long lines of ponies, loaded with buffalo-meat and all the baggage of an Indian hunting-camp, was really a wide strip of very rough country, full of mountains and rising to a high range in the centre. The Lipans were not very well acquainted with it, except by what they had heard from others, and there had been some murmuring among them at first, when their leader announced his intention of following his "war-path" to the other side of such a barrier as that.

His speech had settled it all, however, and his warriors were ready to go with him no matter where he should lead them. Anything rather than go back empty-handed to be laughed at.

The moment luncheon was over every man was on horseback. It was absolutely necessary to find "grass" before night, if their horses were to be good for anything the next day.

They knew that the particular band of Apaches they were pursuing must be two or three days' march ahead of them;

but they also knew that every mountain range has its deep, green valleys, and that the trail left by their enemies would surely lead through the best of these.

Up, up, up, through rugged ravines and gorges for nearly an hour, and then down again almost as far, and then, sooner than they had expected, they came upon the very thing they were looking for. It was not so large or so beautiful a valley as the one in which Many Bears and his men were encamped, miles and miles beyond. It did not widen like that at its lower end into a broad and undulating plain, with a river and a forest far away; but there was plenty of grass in it for tired and hungry horses, and To-la-go-to-de at once decided that there they should halt for the night.

It was little beyond the middle of the afternoon, and a war-party of Lipans has neither tents to pitch nor much baggage to care for. Little time was lost in mere "going into camp," and even before that was done every fifth brave was ordered out to look for game. Not only would fresh meat be better than dry, if they could get any, but it would save their somewhat slender stock of provisions for another day.

"Steve! Steve Harrison!"

"What is it, Murray?"

"I've spoken to old Two Knives. You and I are to hunt."

"Hurrah for that! Which way are you going?"

"Most of the others seem to be setting out southerly. I guess they're right, so far as game is concerned. You and I'll try that gap to the north-west. There's no telling where it may lead to."

The "gap" he pointed at was a sombre-looking chasm, the mouth of which opened into the little valley where they were, at a distance of about half a mile.

Nobody could tell, indeed, where it might lead to, nor could any one have guessed, until he was actually in it, what a very remarkable gap it was.

The two white hunters, little as they looked like white men, had chosen to go on foot, and not one of their Lipan friends had accompanied them. If they were men to be "watched" at any other time, even the sharp eyes of Indian suspicion saw no need for it among the desolate solitudes of those "sierras."

They did not hear To-la-go-to-de say to some of the red hunters:

"No Tongue great hunter. Bring in more antelope than anybody else. Yellow Head good, too. You beat them? Ugh!"

They would try beyond doubt, but more than one Lipan shook his head. The reputation of Murray as a slayer of game was too high to be questioned, and he had taught Steve Harrison like a father.

"Murray," said Steve, "do you mean that such a gap as that offers me a chance?"

"To get away?"

"Yes. That's what I'm thinking of."

"Can't say about that, my boy. Probably not. I don't believe it comes out on the western slope of the mountains."

"What do you want to try it for, then?"

"I don't exactly know. Game, perhaps. Then I want to teach you something more about mountains and finding your way among them. More than that, I don't want to go the same way with any of the rest."

"I like that, anyhow. Seems as if I had ever so many questions to ask that I never felt like asking before."

"I never cared to answer any, Steve, when you did ask 'em. Not so long as you and I were to be together. Now you're going away from me, pretty soon, I don't mind telling some things."

"Going away? Do you mean to say you won't go too? Shall you stay and be a Lipan?"

"You'll go alone, Steve, when you go. That's all."

"Why won't you go with me?"

"That's one of the questions I don't mean to answer. You've told me all about your family and people. I'll know where to look for you if I ever come out into the settlements."

"I wish you'd come. You're a white man. You're not a Mexican either. You're American."

"No, I'm not."

"Not an American?"

"No, Steve, I'm an Englishman. I never told you that before. One reason I don't want to go back is the very thing that sent me down into Mexico to settle years and years ago."

"I didn't ask about that."

"No good if you did."

"But you've been a sort of father to me ever since you bought me from the Lipans, after they cleaned out my uncle's hunting-party, and I can't bear the thought of leaving you here."

If it had not been for his war-paint, and its contrast with his Saxon hair and eyes, Steve would have been a handsome, pleasant-looking boy—tall and strong for his years, but still a good deal of a boy—and his voice was now trembling in a very un-Indian sort of way. No true Lipan would have dreamed of betraying any emotion at parting from even so good a friend as Murray.

"Yes," said the latter, dryly, "they cleaned out the hunting-party. Your uncle and his men must have run pretty well, for not one of them lost his scalp or drew a bead on a Lipan. That's one reason they didn't knock you on the head. They came home laughing, and sold you to me for six ponies and a pipe."

"I never blamed my uncle. I've always wondered, though, what sort of a story he told my father and mother."

"Guess he doesn't amount to a great deal."

"He's rich enough, and he's fond of hunting, but there isn't a great deal of fight in him. He wouldn't make a good Lipan."

The circumstances of Steve's capture were evidently not very creditable to some of those who were concerned in it, and Murray's tone, in speaking of the "uncle" who had brought him out into the Texas plains to lose him so easily, was bitterly contemptuous.

At that moment they were entering the mouth of the gap, and Murray suddenly dropped all other subjects to exclaim,

"We've struck it, Steve!"

"Struck what?"

"A regular canyon. See, the walls are almost perpendicular, and the bottom comes down, from ledge to ledge, like a flight of stairs!"

Steve had been among mountains before, but he had never seen anything precisely like that.

In some places the vast chasm before him was hardly more than a hundred feet wide, while its walls of gray granite and glittering white quartz rock arose in varying heights of from three hundred to five hundred feet.

"Come on, Steve!"

"You won't find any game in here. A rabbit couldn't get enough to live on among such rocks as these."

"Come right along! I want to get a look at the ledges up there. There's no telling what we may stumble upon."

Steve's young eyes were fully occupied, as they pushed forward, with the strange beauty and grandeur of the scenery above, beyond, and behind him. The air was clear and almost cool, and there was plenty of light in the shadiest nooks of the chasm.

"What torrents of water must pour down through here at

some seasons of the year," he was saying to himself, when his companion suddenly stopped, with a sharp, "Hist! Look there!" and raised his rifle.

Steve looked.

Away up on the edge of the beetling white crag at their right, the first "game" they had seen that day was calmly gazing down upon them.

A "big-horn antelope" has the best nerves in the world, and it is nothing to him how high may be the precipice on the edge of which he is standing. His head never gets dizzy, and his feet never slip, for he was made to live in that kind of country, and feels entirely at home in spots where no other living thing cares to follow him.

That was a splendid specimen of what the first settlers called the "Rocky Mountain sheep," until they found that it was not a sheep at all, but an "antelope." His strong, wide, curling horns were of the largest size, and gave him an expression of dignity and wisdom as he peered down upon the hunters who had intruded upon his solitudes. He would have shown more wisdom by not looking at all, for in a moment more the sharp crack of Murray's rifle awoke the echoes of the canyon, and then, with a great bound, the big-horn came tumbling down among the rocks, almost at Steve Harrison's feet.

"He's a little battered by his fall," said Murray, "that's a fact. But he'll be just as good eating. Let's hoist him on that bowlder and go ahead."

"He's as much as we'd like to carry in."

"That's so; but we may bag something more, and then we could bring a pony up almost as far as this. I don't mean to do any too much carrying."

His broad, muscular frame looked as if it had been built expressly for that purpose, and he could have picked up at least one big-horn with perfect ease; but he had been among the Indians a good while, and they never lift a pound more than they are compelled to.

"Give me the next shot, Murray."

"I will, if it's all right; but you must use your own eyes. It won't do to throw away any chances."

The game was quickly lifted to the bowlder pointed out by Murray, and he and Steve pressed on up the great beautiful gate-way, deeper and deeper into the secrets of the mountain range.

Every such range has its secrets, and one by one they are found out from time to time; but there seemed to be little use in the discovery of any just then and there. It was a very useless sort of secret.

What was it?

Well, it was one that had been kept by that deep chasm for nobody could guess how many thousands of years, until Steve Harrison stumbled a little as he climbed one of the broken "stairs" of quartz, and came down upon his hands and knees.

Before him the canyon widened into a sort of table-land, with crags and peaks around it, and Murray saw trees here and there, and a good many other things, but Steve exclaimed,

William O. Stoddard

"Murray! Murray! Gold!"

"What! A vein?"

"I fell right down upon it. Just look there!"

Murray looked, half carelessly at first, like a man who had before that day discovered plenty of such things; but then he sprung forward.

"We're in the gold country," he said; "it's all gold-bearing quartz hereaway. Steve! Steve! I declare I never saw such a vein as that. The metal stands out in nuggets."

So it did. A strip of rock nearly five feet wide was dotted and spangled with bits of dull yellow. It seemed to run right across the canyon at the edge of that level, and disappear in the solid cliffs on either side.

"Oh, what a vein!"

"It's really gold, then?"

"Gold? Of course it is. But it isn't of any use."

"Why not?"

"Who could mine for it away down here in the Apache country? How could they get machinery down here? Why, a regiment of soldiers couldn't keep off the redskins, and every pound of gold would cost two pounds before you could get it to a mint."

For all that, Murray gazed and gazed at the glittering rock, with its scattered jewels of yellow, and a strange light began to glow in his sunken eyes.

"No, Steve, I'm too old for it now. Gold's nothing to me any more! But that ledge is yours, now you've found it. Some day you may come back for it."

"I will if I live, Murray."

"Well, if you ever do, I'll tell you one thing more."

"What's that?"

"Dig and wash in the sand and gravel of that canyon below for all the loose gold that's been washed down there from this ledge since the world was made. There must be bushels of it."

CHAPTER V

The lodge of tanned buffalo-skins in which Ni-ha-be and Rita were sitting with Mother Dolores, was large and commodious. It was a round tent, upheld by strong, slender poles, that came together at the top so as to leave a small opening. On the outside the covering was painted in bright colors with a great many rude figures of men and animals. There was no furniture; but some buffalo and bear skins and some blankets were spread upon the ground, and it was a very comfortable lodge for any weather that was likely to come in that region.

In such a bright day as that all the light needed came through the open door, for the "flap" was still thrown back.

The two girls, therefore, could see every change on the dark face of the great chiefs Mexican squaw.

A good many changes came, for Dolores was very busily "remembering," and it was full five minutes before the thoughts brought to her by that picture of the "Way-side Shrine" began to fade away, so that she was again an Indian.

"Rita," whispered Ni-ha-be, "did it say anything to you?"

"Yes. A little. I saw something like it long ago. But I don't know what it means."

"Rita! Ni-ha-be!"

"What is it, Dolores?"

"Go. You will be in my way. I must cook supper for the chief. He is hungry. You must not go beyond the camp."

"What did the talking leaf say to you?" asked Ni-ha-be.

"Nothing. It is a great medicine leaf. I shall keep it. Perhaps it will say more to Rita by-and-by. Go."

The Apaches, like other Indians, know very little about cookery. They can roast meat and broil it, after a fashion, and they have several ways of cooking fish. They know how to boil when they are rich enough to have kettles, and they can make a miserable kind of corn-bread with Indian corn, dried or parched and pounded fine.

The one strong point in the character of Dolores, so far as the good opinion of old Many Bears went, was that she was the best cook in his band. She had not quite forgotten some things of that kind that she had learned before she became a squaw. Nobody else, therefore, was permitted to cook supper for the hungry chief.

It was a source of many jealousies among his other squaws, but then he was almost always hungry, and none of them knew how to cook as she did.

She was proud of it too, and neither Ni-ha-be nor her adopted sister dreamed of disputing with her after she had uttered the word "supper."

They hurried out of the lodge, therefore, and Dolores was left alone. She had no fire to kindle.

That would be lighted in the open air by other female members of the family.

There were no pots and saucepans to be washed, although the one round, shallow, sheet-iron "fryer," such as soldiers sometimes use in camp, which she dragged from under a buffalo-skin in the corner, would have been none the worse for a little scrubbing.

She brought it out, and then she dropped it and sat down to take another look at that wonderful "talking leaf."

"What made me kneel down and shut my eyes? I could remember then. It is all gone now. It went away as soon as I got up again."

She folded the leaf carefully, and hid it in the folds of her deer-skin dress, but she was evidently a good deal puzzled.

"Maria Santissima—yes, I do remember that. It will all come back to me by-and-by. No! I don't want it to. It makes me afraid. I will cook supper and forget all about it."

A Mexican woman of the lower class, unable to read, ignorant of almost everything but a little plain cookery, has less to forget than have most American children of six years old. But why should it frighten her if the little she knew and had lost began to come back to her mind?

She did not stop to answer any such questions as that, but poured some pounded corn, a coarse, uneven meal, into a battered tin pan. To this was added a little salt, some water was stirred in till a thick paste was made, and then the best cook of the Apaches was ready to carry her batter to the fire. Envious black eyes watched her while she heated her saucepan on the coals she raked out. Then she melted a carefully measured piece of buffalo tallow, and began to fry for her husband and master the cakes no other of his squaws could so well prepare.

When the cakes were done brown, the same fryer and a little water would serve to take the toughness out of some strips of dried venison before she broiled them, and the great chief would be the best-fed man in camp until the hunters should return from the valley below with fresh game.

They were quite likely to do that before night, but Many Bears was a man who never waited long for something to eat after a hard day's march.

If Dolores had been a little alarmed at the prospect of being forced to "remember," a very different feeling had entered the mind of Rita when she and her sister came out of the lodge.

"What shall we do, Ni-ha-be?"

"Red Wolf told me he had something to say to me. There he is now. He beckons me to come. He does not want you."

"I am glad of it. There are trees and bushes down there beyond the corral. I will go and be alone."

"You will tell me all the talking leaves say to you?"

"Yes, but they will talk very slowly, I'm afraid."

Even the harsher sounds of the Apache tongue had a pleasant ring in the sweet, clear voices of the two girls, and the softer syllables, of which there were many, rippled after each other like water in a brook. It seemed, too, as if they said quite as much to each other by signs as by words. That is always so among people who live a great deal out-of-doors, or in narrow quarters, where other people can easily hear ordinary conversation.

The one peculiar thing about the signs used by the American Indians is that they mean so much and express it so clearly. Men of different tribes, not able to understand a word of each other's spoken tongue, will meet and talk together by the hour in "sign language" as intelligently as two well-trained deaf mutes among the whites.

Perhaps one reason more for so much "sign talking" is that there are so many tribes, each with a very rough tongue of its own, that is not easy for other tribes to pick up.

Red Wolf was again beckoning to Ni-ha-be, and there was an impatient look on his dark, self-willed face. It was time for her to make haste, therefore, and Rita put the three magazines under the light folds of her broad antelope-skin cap and tripped away toward the bit of bushy grove just beyond the "corral."

What is that?

In the language of the very "far West" it is any spot or place where horses are gathered and kept, outside of a stable.

The great Apache nation does not own a single stable or barn, although it does own multitudes of horses, ponies, mules, and even horned cattle. All these, therefore, have to be "corralled," except when they are running loose among their unfenced pastures. There are no fences in that part of the world any more than barns.

Immediately on going into camp the long train of pack mules and ponies had been relieved of their burdens, and they and most of the saddle-horses had been sent off, under the care of mounted herders, to pick their dinners for themselves in the rich green grass of the valley.

Chiefs and warriors, however, never walk if they can help it, and so, as some one of them might wish to go here or there at any moment, several dozens of the freshest animals were kept on the spot between the camp and the grove, tethered by long hide lariats, and compelled to wait their turn for something to eat.

There was a warrior on guard at the "corral," as a matter of course, but he hardly gave a glance to the pretty adopted daughter of Many Bears as she tripped hurriedly past him.

It was his business to look out for the horses and not for giddy young squaws who might find "talking leaves."

Rita could not have told him, if he had asked her, why it was that her prizes were making her heart beat so fast, as she held them against it.

She was not frightened. She knew that very well. But she was glad to be alone, without even the company of Ni-ha-be.

The bushes were very thick around the spot where she at last threw herself upon the grass. She had never lived in any lodge where there were doors to shut behind her, or if she had, all those houses and their doors were alike forgotten; but she knew that her quick ears would give her notice of any approaching footsteps.

There they lay now before her, the three magazines, and it seemed to Rita as if they had come on purpose to see her, and were looking at her.

No two of them were alike.

They did not even belong to the same family. She could tell that by their faces.

Slowly and half-timidly she turned the first leaf; it was the cover-leaf of the nearest.

A sharp exclamation sprung to her lips.

"I have seen her! Oh, so long ago! It is me, Rita. I wore a dress like that once. And the tall squaw behind her, with the robe that drags on the ground, I remember her, too. How did they know she was my mother?"

Rita's face had been growing very white, and now she covered it with both her hands and began to cry. The picture was one of a fine-looking lady and a little girl of, it might be, seven or eight years. Not Rita and her mother, surely, for the lady wore a coronet upon her head and carried a sceptre in her hand; but the little girl looked very much as Rita must have looked at her age. It was a picture of some Spanish princess and her daughter, but like many pictures of such people that are printed, it would have served as well for a portrait of almost anybody else—particularly, as it seemed, of Rita and her mother.

"He is not there. Why did they not put him in? I love him best. Oh, he was so good to me! He had plenty of talking leaves, too, and he taught them to speak to me. I will look and see if he is here."

Rita was talking aloud to herself, but her own voice sounded strange to her, with its Indian words and ways of expression.

She was listening, without knowing it, for another voice—for several of them—and none of them spoke Apache.

She turned leaf after leaf with fluttering haste, in her eager search for that other face she had spoken of.

In a moment more she paused, as the full-length picture of a man gazed at her from the paper.

"No; not him. He is too old. My father was not old; and he was handsome, and he was not dark at all."

She shut the book for a moment, and her face was full of puzzle and of pain.

"I said it. I was not talking Apache then. And I understood what I was saying."

She had indeed, when she mentioned her father, spoken pretty clearly in English.

Was it her mother-tongue? and had it come back to her?

She turned over the leaves more eagerly than ever now, and she found in that and the two other magazines many pictured faces of men of all ages, but each one brought her a fresh disappointment.

"He is not here," she said, mournfully; "and it was he who taught me to—to—to read—read books."

She had found two words now that were like little windows, for through them she could see a world of wonderful things that she had not seen before.

"Read" and "books."

The three magazines were no longer "talking leaves" to her, although they were really beginning to talk. Her head ached, and her eyes were burning hot, as she gazed so intently at word after word of the page which happened to be open before her. It was not printed like the rest—less closely, and not in such a thronging mass of little black spots of letters. It was a piece of very simple poetry, in short lines and brief stanzas, and Rita was staring at its title.

The letters slowly came to her one by one, bringing behind them the first word of the title; but they seemed to Rita to be in her own brain more than on the paper.

It was a hard moment for Rita.

"He made me say them one word at a time. He was so good to me! Yes, I can say them now! I know what they mean! Oh, so long ago! so long ago!"

There was no longer any doubt about it. Rita could read English.

Not very easily or rapidly at first, and many of the words she came to puzzled her exceedingly. Perhaps some of them also would come back to her after a while. Some of them had always been strangers, for the very brightest little girls of seven or eight, even when they read well and have their fathers to help them, are but at the beginning of their acquaintance with "hard words."

"I shall know what the pictures mean now. But I will not tell anybody a word about it—only Ni-ha-be."

CHAPTER VI

Steve Harrison rose to his feet, and looked curiously along the ledge in both directions.

It was not the first ore he had seen during his three years and more of wandering with Murray and the Lipans, but never before had he tumbled down upon anything precisely like it.

"Mine!" he said to himself, aloud—"mine! But what can I do with it?"

"Do with it? What can you do with it?"

Murray was still kneeling upon the precious quartz, and fingering spot after spot where the yellow metal showed itself; and the strange fire in his eyes was deeper than ever.

"Steve!"

"What, Murray?"

"I thought it was all gone, but it isn't."

"Thought what was all gone?"

"The gold-fever. I used to have it when I was younger. It isn't

William O. Stoddard

a love of money. It's just a love of digging up gold."

"Can you feel it now?"

"Dreadfully. It burns all over me every time I touch one of those nuggets."

"Let it burn, then."

"Why? What's the good of it?"

"Maybe it'll get strong enough to keep you from wasting the rest of your days among the Lipans."

"Among the Lipans? You don't know, Steve. Didn't I tell you what keeps me? No, I don't think I did—not all of it. You're only a boy, Steve."

"You're a wonderfully strong man for your age."

"My age? How old do you think I am?"

"I never guessed. Maybe you're not much over sixty."

"Sixty?" He said that with a sort of low laugh.

"Why, my dear boy, I'm hardly turned of forty-five—white hair and all. The white came to my hair the day I spent in hunting among the ruins the Apaches left behind them for my wife and my little girl."

"Only forty-five! Why, Murray, you're young yet. And you know all about mines."

"And all about Indians too. Come on, Steve; we must look a little farther before we set out for the camp."

Steve would willingly have stayed to look at all that useless ledge of gold ore; but his friend was on his feet again, now resolutely turning his wrinkled face away from it all, and there was nothing to be gained be mere gazing. A gold-mine cannot be worked by a person's eyes, even if they are as good and bright a pair as were those of Steve Harrison.

Before them lay the broken level of the table-land, and it was clearer and clearer, as they walked on, that it was not at all a desert.

It was greater in extent, too, than appeared at first sight, and it was not long before their march brought them to quite a grove of trees.

"Oak and maple, I declare," said Murray. "I'd hardly have thought of finding them here. There's good grass too, beyond, and running water."

"Halloo, Murray, what's that? Look! Are they houses?"

"Steve! Steve!"

It was no wonder at all that they both broke into a clean run, and that they did not halt again until they stood in the edge of a second grove not far from the margin of the full-banked stream of water which wound down from the mountains and ran across that plateau.

Trees, groves, grass, in all directions, and a herd of deer were feeding at no great distance, but it was not at any of these that the two "pale-faced Lipans" were gazing.

"Houses, Murray!—houses!"

"They were houses once, Steve. Good ones, too. I've heard of

William O. Stoddard

such before. These are not like what I've seen in Mexico."

"They're all in ruins. Some one has started a settlement here and had to give it up. Maybe they came to work my mine."

It was less than half an hour since he had stumbled over it, and yet Steve was already thinking of that ledge as "my mine."

It does not take us a great while to acquire a feeling of ownership for anything we take a great liking to.

"Settlement! Work your mine!" exclaimed Murray. "Why, Steve, the people that built those houses were all dead and gone before even the Apaches came here. Nobody knows who they were. Not even the wisest men in the world."

That was a great relief to Steve, for if they had been forgotten so completely as that they were sure not to interfere with him and his mine.

The two friends walked forward again until they stood in the shadow of the nearest ruin.

It must have been a pretty large building before its walls began to topple over with age and decay. Some parts that were yet standing were three stories high, and all was built of rudely shaped and roughly fitted stone. There was no mortar to be seen anywhere. If there had ever been any it was all washed away.

"There must have been quite a town here once," said Murray, "up and down both banks of the run of water. It was a good place for one. It looks as if there was plenty of good land beyond, and there's a great bend in the line of the mountains."

"I wish I knew where it led to. I'd follow it."

"What for?"

"It might give me a chance to get away."

"It might. And then again it might not. There's a gap that seems to open off there to the west, but then it won't do."

"Why won't it do? Couldn't I try it?"

"Try it? Yes, but you won't. I must look out for you, Steve. You're more of a boy than I thought for."

"I'm man enough, Murray. I dare try anything."

"That's boy, Steve. Stop a minute. Have you any horse to carry you across country?"

Steve looked down at the nearest pile of ruined masonry with a saddening face.

"You have no horse, no blanket, no provisions, no supply of ammunition except what you brought along for to-day's hunt. Why, Steve, I'm ashamed of you. There isn't a young Lipan brave in the whole band that would set off in such a fashion as that—sure to make a failure. You ought to have learned something from the Indians, it seems to me."

Steve blushed scarlet as he listened, for he had been ready the moment before to have shouldered his rifle and set off at once toward that vague and unknown western "gap." It must be that the glimpse he had taken of that golden ledge had stirred up all the "boy" in him.

"I guess I wouldn't have gone far," he said, "before I'd have run clean out of cartridges. I've less than two dozen with me."

"When you do start, my boy, I'll see to it that you get a good ready. Now let's try for one of those deer. It's a long shot. See if you can make it."

A fine buck with branching antlers, followed by two does, had been feeding in the open space beyond the ruins. The wind was brisk just then from that direction, and they had not scented the two hunters. They had slowly drawn nearer and nearer until they were now about three hundred yards away. That is a greater distance than is at all safe shooting for any but the best marksmen, and sometimes even they will lose their game at it.

The stories so often told of "long shots" at deer and tigers and geese and other terrible wild beasts are, for the greater part, of the kind that are known as "fish stories," and Steve would have been glad if that buck had been a few rods nearer.

He knew his rifle was a good one, however, for it was a seven-shooting repeater of the latest and best pattern, and had been selected for him by Murray himself out of a lot the Lipans had brought in, nobody knew from where.

"Steady, Steve! Think of the deer, not of the gold-mine."

"I'll aim at him as if he were a gold-mine," replied Steve, as he raised his rifle.

"I'll try for one of the does at the same time," said Murray.

Crack! crack! Both rifles were discharged almost at the same instant; but while the antlered buck gave a great bound and then fell motionless upon the grass, his two pretty companions sprung away unhurt.

"I aimed too high," said Murray; "I must lower my sights a little."

"I've got him," exclaimed Steve—"gold-mine and all; but he'll be a big load to carry to camp."

They found him so. They were compelled to take more than one breathing-spell before they reached the head of the ravine, and there they took a long one—right on the gold-bearing ledge.

"Splendid pair of horns he has—" began Murray, but Steve interrupted him with,

"That's it! That's the name of this mine when I come for it!"

"What's that, Steve?"

"It's the Buckhorn Mine. They always give them a name."

"That'll do as well as any. The ledge'll stay here till you come for it. Nobody around here is likely to steal it away from you. But there's more ledge than mine just now."

So there was, and Steve's countenance fell a little as he and Murray again took up their burden and began to toil under it from "stair to stair" down the rocky terraces of the grand chasm.

"We won't go any farther than we can help without a horse," said Murray at last. "And there's the big-horn to carry in."

"Murray, that big-horn! Just look yonder!"

It was not far to look, and the buck they were carrying seemed to come to the ground of his own accord.

"Cougar!" exclaimed Murray.

"The biggest painter I ever saw," said Steve, "and he is getting ready to spring."

The American panther, or, as Murray called him, cougar, is not so common among the mountains as he is in some parts of the forest-covered lowlands, but the vicinity of the table-land above, with its herds of deer, might account for this one. There he was now, at all events, preparing to take possession of the game on the top of that bowlder without asking leave of anybody.

"Quick, Steve! Forward, while he's got his eyes on the antelope. We may get a shot at him."

Almost recklessly they darted down the canyon, slipping swiftly along from bowlder to bowlder, but before they had covered half the distance the panther made his spring.

He made it magnificently. He had scented the blood of that antelope from far away, and he may have suspected that it was not a living one, but his instincts had forbidden him to approach it otherwise than with caution. He would not have been a cougar if he had not made a spring in seizing upon his prey.

They are nothing in the world but giant cats, after all, and they catch their game precisely as our house-cats catch their mice. If anybody wants to know how even a lion or a tiger does his hunting, "puss in the corner" can teach him all about it.

"He will tear it all to pieces!"

"No, he won't, Steve. We can get a bead on him from behind that rock yonder. He'll be too busy to be looking out for us for a minute or so."

That was true, and it was a bad thing for the great "cat of the mountains" that it was so, for the two hunters got within a hundred yards of him before he had done smelling of the big-horn, in which he had buried his sharp, terrible claws.

"Now, Steve, I won't miss my shot this time. See that you don't."

Steve took even too much care with his aim, and Murray fired first.

He did not miss; but a cougar is not like a deer, and it takes a good deal more to kill him. Murray's bullet struck a vital part, and the fierce beast sprung from the bowlder with a ferocious growl of sudden pain and anger.

"I hit him! Quick, Steve!"

The panther was crouching on the gravel at the bottom of the ravine, and searching with furious eyes for the enemies who had wounded him.

The report of Steve's rifle rung through the chasm.

"I aimed at his head—"

"And you only cut off one of his ears. Here he comes. I'm ready. What a good thing a repeating-rifle is!"

It was well for them, indeed, that they did not have to stop and load just then. It did not seem any time at all before the dangerous beast was crouching for another spring within

William O. Stoddard

twenty feet of them.

It would not do to miss this time, but neither Steve nor Murray made any remarks about it. They were too much absorbed in looking along their rifle-barrels to do any talking. Both reports came together, almost like one.

They were not followed by any spring from the cougar. Only by a growl and an angry tearing at the gravel, and then there was no danger that any more big-horns, living or dead, would ever be stolen by that panther.

"Well, Steve, if this isn't the biggest kind of sport! Never saw anything better in all my life."

"A buck, a big-horn, and a painter before sundown!"

"It'll be sundown before we get them all in. We'd better start for some ponies and some help. Tell you what, Steve, I don't care much for it myself, but the Lipans would rather eat that cougar than the best venison ever was killed."

"I suppose they would; but I ain't quite Indian enough for that, war-paint or no war-paint."

So, indeed, it proved; and To-la-go-to-de indulged in more than one sarcastic gibe at his less successful hunters over the manner in which they had been beaten by "No Tongue and the Yellow Head—an old pale-face and a boy." He even went so far as to say to Steve Harrison, "Good shot. The Yellow Head will be a chief some day. He must kill many Apaches. Ugh!"

CHAPTER VII

When Steve Harrison and his friend left the ruins of the ancient town behind them, they had good reason to suppose that they were going away from a complete solitude—a place where even wild Indians did not very often come.

It looked desolate enough with its scattered enclosures of rough stone, not one of them with any roof on, or any sign that people had lived in them for a hundred years at least. The windows in the tumbling walls had probably never had either sash or glass in them, and the furniture, whatever it may have been, used by the people who built the village had long since disappeared.

It could never have been a very large or populous town, but it could hardly at any time have had a wilder-looking set of inhabitants than were the party of men who drew near it at about the time when Steve and Murray were killing their cougar.

Two tilted wagons, a good deal the worse for wear, apparently pretty heavily laden, and drawn by six mules each, were accompanied by about two dozen men on horseback. Their portraits would have made the fortune of any picture-gallery in the world. Everybody would have gone to look at such a collection of bearded desperadoes.

They were not Indians, nor were they dressed as such. They were dressed in every way that could be thought of, except well and cleanly.

If the odds and ends of several clothing-stores had been picked up after a fire, and then about worn out, and patched and mended with bits of blankets and greasy buckskin, something like those twenty odd suits of clothes might have been produced; that is, if the man who tried to do it could have had these for a pattern. If not, he would have failed.

The men themselves were as much out of the common way as were the clothes they wore, but they had somehow managed to keep their horses and mules in pretty good condition.

Horses and mules are of more importance than clothing to men who are far away from tailors and civilization as were these new-comers in the neighborhood of Steve's mine.

If Steve had seen them he would probably have trembled for the "Buckhorn," for Murray would at once have told him that these men were miners.

That was nothing against them, certainly, and they must have been daring fellows to push their hunt for gold so far beyond any region known to such hunters.

One look at their hard, reckless faces would have convinced anybody about their "daring." They looked as if they were ready for anything.

So they were, indeed; and it is quite probable a man of Murray's experience would have guessed at once that they were ready for a good many other things besides mining.

Just now, certainly, they were thinking something else.

"Bill," said the foremost rider to a man a little behind him, "we were wrong to leave the trail of them army fellers. We're stuck and lost in here among the mountains."

"It looks like It. We'll hev to go into camp and scout around till we find a pass. But it wasn't any use follerin' the cavalry arter we found they was bound west."

"That's so. It won't do for us to come out on the Pacific slope. It's Mexico or Texas for us."

"We'd better say Santa Fe."

"They'd make us give too close an account of ourselves there. Some of the boys might let out somethin'."

"Guess it's Mexico, then. That isn't far away now. But I wish I knew the way down out of this."

The ruins, strange and wonderful as they were, did not seem to excite any great degree of curiosity among those men.

They talked about them, to be sure, but in a way which showed that they had all seen the same sort of thing before during their wild rovings among the mountains and valleys of the great South-west.

Just such ruins are to be found in a great many places. We do not even know how many, and nobody has been able yet to more than guess by whom they were built or when.

Mere ravines and gorges and canyons would not do for this party. They must find a regular "pass," down which they could manage to take their horses and mules and wagons.

William O. Stoddard

Even before they halted, several of them had been looking and pointing toward what Murray had spoken of as "the western gap."

That was the opening through the ranges which had been for a moment such a temptation to Steve Harrison.

"It's west'ard, Bill, but it may hev to do for us."

"It may take us down to some lower level, or it may show us a way south."

"The great Southern Pass is down hereaway, somewhar."

"Farther east than this. We ort to strike it, though, before we cross the border."

"Mexico ain't a country I'd choose to go inter, ef I hed my own way; but we've got to go for it this time."

But whatever may have been their reason for seeking Mexico, they were just now a good deal puzzled as to the precise path by means of which they might reach it. It was getting late in the day, too, for any kind of exploration, and the mule-teams looked as if they had done about enough.

So it came to pass that the ruined village of the forgotten people was once more occupied.

Did they go into the houses? No, it was the man called Bill who said it, but all the rest of them seemed to feel just as he did, when he remarked:

"Sleep in one of them things? No, I guess not. Not even if it was roofed in. They were set up too long ago to suit me."

That stamped him as an American, for there is no other people in the world that hate old houses. No real American was ever known to use an old building of any kind a day longer than he could help. He would as soon think of wearing old clothes just because they were old.

The ground near the ruins was covered with fragments of stone and fallen masonry, but there was a good camping-ground between that and the trees from which Murray and Steve had fired at the buck.

"It's the loneliest kind of a place, Captain Skinner," said Bill, just after he had helped turn the mules loose on the grass.

"I wish I knew just how lonely it is. I kind o' smell something."

"Do ye, Cap?"

Every such band of men has its "Captain" of some kind, and sometimes very good discipline and order is kept up. But Captain Skinner was hardly the man anybody would have picked out for a leader, before seeing how the rest listened to what he said, and how readily they seemed to obey him.

He was the shortest, thinnest, ugliest, and most ragged man in the whole party; and just at this moment he did not appear to be carrying any arms except the knife and pistol in his belt.

"If I don't smell it, I can see it. Look yonder, Bill."

"That's so! Blood!"

It was the spot on which the buck had fallen, and in a moment more than half a dozen men were looking around in all directions.

They understood all they saw, too, as well as any Indians in the world, for in less than five minutes Captain Skinner said,

"That'll do, boys. We must follow that trail. Two white hunters. They killed the buck. Both wore moccasins. So they ain't fresh from the settlements. There's something queer about it. They were on foot, and they carried off their game."

It was, indeed, very queer, and it would not do to let any such puzzle as that go by unsolved.

So, while several men were ordered out after game, and several more were left to guard the camp, Captain Skinner himself, with Bill and five others, armed to the teeth, set out at once on the trail of Murray and Steve Harrison.

It was easy enough to follow those two pairs of footprints as long as they were made in the grass. After they got upon rocky ground it was not so easy, and the miners did not get ahead so fast, but they did not lose the trail for a moment. Indeed, it was about as straight in one direction as the nature of the ground would permit.

"Two fellers out yer among these 'ere mountains all by themselves," growled Bill, as they drew near the ledge at the head of the deep canyon.

"We don't know that they're all alone yet," said Captain Skinner. "They carried that deer somewhere."

"Right down yonder, Captain. They stopped here to rest from kerryin' of it, and I don't blame 'em, if they'd got to tote it down through that thar canyon."

"It's a deep one, no mistake."

"Captain, look yer!" suddenly exclaimed one of the men. "We've lit on it this time."

"The ledge? I wasn't looking at that."

A perfect storm of exclamations followed from every pair of lips in the party. Such a ledge as that they had never seen before, old mine-hunters as they were; but each one seemed inclined to ask, just as Murray had asked of Steve, what could be done with it?

Gold enough, but nothing to get it out of the rock with, and nowhere to carry it to.

It was a sad problem for men who cared for nothing in the wide world but just such ledges and just such gold. What was the use of it?

Steve Harrison never knew it, but his mine was of a good deal of use to him and Murray just then. It kept Captain Skinner and his men looking at it long enough for them to get nearly back to the camp of the Lipans.

"It won't do, boys," said Captain Skinner, at last; "we're wasting time. Come on."

They followed him, every man turning his head as he did so to take another look at the yellow spots that shone here and there in the quartz.

Their way down the ravine was made with care and circumspection, for they did not know at what moment they might come in sight of "those two fellers and their deer."

It was well for them, probably, that they were cautious, for after a good deal of steep climbing, just as they were about to clamber down one of the rocky "stairs," the man called Bill exclaimed,

"Captain, thar it is—"

"The deer? They've left it. I see it."

"More'n that farther down."

"A big-horn! And if that ain't a painter lying beside it!"

"More'n that, Cap. They didn't give up that thar game for nothin'."

"Lay low, boys! Git to cover right away! Red-skins!"

There was no difficulty in hiding among so many rocks and bowlders, and the miners were out of sight in a moment.

They could see, though, even if they were not seen, and they were soon able to count a dozen Indian warriors leading three pack-ponies as far up the ravine as four-footed beasts could be led.

"Wonder if they've wiped out the two fellers?" said Bill.

"Looks like it. Or they may have captured 'em. Lost their game, if they haven't lost their scalps. Wonder what tribe of redskins they are, anyhow?"

There was a better reason than that why No Tongue and Yellow Head did not come back with their friends, but it was just as well that Captain Skinner and his miners did not understand it.

"Captain," whispered one of the men near him, "shall we let drive at 'em? We could pick off half of 'em first fire."

"Not a shot. All we want just now is to be let alone. I don't mind killing a few redskins."

"Mebbe they killed the two fellers."

"Likely as not. I'm kind o' glad they did. That there ledge is ours now. Let 'em carry off their game, and then we'll climb back. I reckon I know now how we'd best work our way down to the level those Indians came from."

The Lipans made short work of loading their ponies, and the moment they were out of sight the miners began their climb out of that canyon. There was no good reason why they should follow the Lipans.

William O. Stoddard

CHAPTER VIII

A refusal to go out with the hunters was a strange thing to come from Red Wolf. No other young brave in that band of Apaches had a better reputation for killing deer and buffaloes. It was a common saying among the older squaws that when he came to have a lodge of his own "there would always be plenty of meat in it."

He was not, therefore, a "lazy Indian," and it was something he had on his mind that kept him in the camp that day. It had also made him beckon to Ni-ha-be, and look very hard after Rita when she hurried away toward the bushes with her three magazines of "talking leaves." Red Wolf was curious.

He hardly liked to say as much to a squaw, even such a young squaw as Ni-ha-be, and his own sister, but he had some questions to ask her, nevertheless.

He might have asked some of them of his father, but the great war-chief of that band of Apaches was now busily watching Dolores and her saucepan, and everybody knew better than to speak to him just before supper.

Ni-ha-be saw at a glance what was the matter with her haughty brother, and she was glad enough to tell him all there was to know of how and where the talking leaves had been found.

"Did they speak to you?"

"No. But I saw pictures."

"Pictures of what?"

"Mountains; big lodges; trees; braves; pale-face squaws; pappooses; white men's bears; and pictures that lied—not like anything."

"Ugh! Bad medicine. Talk too much. So blue-coat soldier throw them away."

"They talk to Rita."

"What say to her?"

"I don't know. She'll tell me. She'll tell you if you ask her."

"Ugh! No. Red Wolf is a warrior. Not want any squaw talk about pictures. You ask Rita some things."

"What things?"

"Make the talking leaves tell where all blue-coat soldiers go. All that camped here. Know then whether we follow 'em."

"Maybe they won't tell."

"Burn some. The rest talk then. White man's leaves not want to tell about white man. Rita must make them talk. Old braves in camp say they know. Many times the talking leaves tell the pale-faces all about Indians. Tell where go. Tell what do. Tell how to find and kill. Bad medicine."

The "old braves" of many an Indian band have puzzled their heads over the white man's way of learning things and sending messages to a distance, and Red Wolf's ideas had nothing unusual in them. If the talking leaves could say anything at all, they could be made to tell a chief and his warriors the precise things they wanted to know.

Ni-ha-be's talk with her brother lasted until he pointed to the camp-fire, where Many Bears was resting after his first attack upon the results of Mother Dolores's cooking.

"Great chief eat. Good time talk to him. Go now."

There was no intentional lack of politeness in the sharp, overbearing tone of Red Wolf. It was only the ordinary manner of a warrior speaking to a squaw. It would therefore have been very absurd for Ni-ha-be to get out of temper about it; but her manner and the toss of her head as she turned away was decidedly wanting in the submissive meekness to be expected of her age and sex.

"It won't be long before I have a lodge of my own," she said, positively. "I'll have Rita come and live with me. Red Wolf shall not make her burn the talking leaves. Maybe she can make them talk to me. My eyes are better than hers. She's nothing but a pale-face, if she did get brought into my father's lodge."

A proud-spirited maiden was Ni-ha-be, and one who wanted a little more of "her own way" than she could have under the iron rule of her great father and the watchful eyes of Mother Dolores.

"I'll go to the bushes and see Rita. Our supper won't be ready yet for a good while."

It would be at least an hour, but Ni-ha-be had never seen a clock in her life, and knew nothing at all about "hours." There is no word for such a thing in the Apache language.

She was as light of foot as an antelope, and her moccasins hardly made a sound upon the grass as she parted the bushes and looked in upon Rita's hiding-place.

"Weeping? The talking leaves have been scolding her! I will burn them! They shall not say things to make her cry!"

In a moment more her arms were around the neck of her adopted sister. It was plain enough that the two girls loved each other dearly.

"Rita, what is the matter? Have they said strong words to you?"

"No, Ni-ha-be; good words, all of them. Only I cannot understand them all."

"Tell me some. See if I can understand them. I am the daughter of a great chief."

Ni-ha-be did not know how very little help the wealth of a girl's father can give her in a quarrel with her school-books. But just such ideas as hers have filled the silly heads of countless young white people of both sexes.

"I can tell you some of it."

"Tell me what made you cry."

"I can't find my father. He is not here. Not in any of them."

"You don't need him now. He was only a pale-face. Many

Bears is a great chief. He is your father now."

Something seemed to tell Rita that she would not be wise to arouse her friend's national jealousy. It was better to turn to some of the pictures and try to explain them. Very funny explanations she gave, too, but she at least knew more than Ni-ha-be, and the latter listened seriously enough.

"Rita, was there ever such a mule as that?—one that could carry a pack under his skin?"

It was Rita's turn now to be proud, for that was one of the pictures she had been able to understand. She had even read enough to be able to tell Ni-ha-be a good deal about a camel.

It was deeply interesting, but the Apache maiden suddenly turned from the page to exclaim,

"Rita, Red Wolf says the talking leaves must tell you about the blue-coat soldiers or he will burn them up."

"I'm going to keep them."

"I won't let him touch them."

"But, Ni-ha-be, they do tell about the soldiers. Look here."

She picked up another of the magazines, and turned over a few leaves.

"There they are. All mounted and ready to march."

Sure enough, there was a fine woodcut of a party of cavalry moving out of camp with wagons.

Over went the page, and there was another picture.

Ten times as many cavalry on the march, followed by an artillery force with cannon.

"Oh, Rita! Father must see that."

"Of course he must; but that is not all."

Another leaf was turned, and there was a view of a number of Indian chiefs in council at a fort, with a strong force of both cavalry and infantry drawn up around them.

Rita had not read the printed matter on any of those pages, and did not know that it was only an illustrated description of campaigning and treaty-making on the Western plains. She was quite ready to agree with Ni-ha-be that Many Bears ought to hear at once what the talking leaves had to say about so very important a matter.

It was a good time to see him now, for he was no longer very hungry, and word had come in from the hunters that they were having good success. A fine prospect of a second supper, better than the first, was just the thing to make the mighty chief good-tempered, and he was chatting cosily with some of his "old braves" when Rita and Ni-ha-be drew near.

They beckoned to Red Wolf first.

"The talking leaves have told Rita all you wanted them to. She must speak to father."

Red Wolf's curiosity was strong enough to make him arrange for that at once, and even Many Bears himself let his face relax into a grim smile as the two girls came timidly nearer the circle of warriors.

After all, they were the pets and favorites of the chief; they

William O. Stoddard

were young and pretty, and so long as they did not presume to know more than warriors and counsellors they might be listened to. Besides, there were the talking leaves, and Rita's white blood, bad as it was for her, might be of some use in such a matter.

"Ugh!"

Many Bears looked at the picture of the cavalry squad with a sudden start. "No lie this time. Camp right here. Just so many blue-coats. Just so many wagons. Good. Now where go?"

Rita turned the leaf, and her Indian father was yet more deeply interested.

"Ugh! More blue-coats. Great many. No use follow. Get all killed. Big guns. Indians no like 'em. Ugh!"

If the cavalry expedition was on its way to join a larger force, it would indeed be of no use to follow it, and Many Bears was a cautious leader as well as a brave one.

Rita's news was not yet all given, however, and when the eyes of the chief fell upon the picture of the "treaty-making" he sprang to his feet.

"Ugh! Big talk come. Big presents. Other Apaches all know—all be there—all get blanket, gun, tobacco, new axe. Nobody send us word, because we off on hunt beyond the mountains. Now we know, we march right along. Rest horse, kill game, then ride. Not lose our share of presents."

Rita could not have told him his mistake; and, even if she had known it, she would have been puzzled to explain away the message of the talking leaves. Did not every brave in the band know that that first picture told the truth about the cavalry? Why, then, should they doubt the correctness of the rest of it?

No, a treaty there was to be, and presents were to come from the red man's "Great Father at Washington," and that band of Apaches must manage to be on hand, and secure all that belonged to it, and as much more as possible.

Red Wolf had nothing more to say about burning up leaves which had talked so well, and his manner toward Rita was almost respectful as he led her and Ni-ha-be away from the group of great men that was now gathering around the chief. Red Wolf was too young a brave to have any business to remain while gray heads were in council. A chief would almost as soon take advice from a squaw as from a "boy."

Mother Dolores had heard nothing of all this, but her eyes had not missed the slightest thing. She had even permitted a large slice of deer-meat to burn to a crisp, in her eager curiosity.

"What did they say to the chief?" was her first question to Rita; but Ni-ha-be answered her with,

"Ask the warriors. If we talk too much we shall get into trouble."

"You must tell me."

"Not till after supper. Rita, don't let's tell her a word unless she cooks for us, and gives us all we want. She made us get our own supper last night."

"You came late. I did not tell your father. I gave you enough. I am very good to you."

"No," said Rita, "sometimes you are cross, and we don't get enough to eat. Now you shall cook us some corn-bread and some fresh meat. I am tired of dried buffalo; it is tough."

The curiosity of Dolores was getting hotter and hotter, and she thought again of the wonderful leaf which had spoken to her. She wanted to ask Rita questions about that, too, and she had learned by experience that there was more to be obtained from her wilful young friends by coaxing than in any other way.

"I will get your supper now, while the chiefs are talking. It shall be a good supper—good enough for Many Bears. Then you shall tell me all I ask."

"Of course I will," said Rita.

A fine fat deer had been deposited near that campfire by one of the first hunters that returned, and Mother Dolores was free to cut and carve from it; but her first attempt at a supper for the girls did not succeed very well. It was not on account of any fault of hers, however, or because the venison-steak she cut and spread upon the coals, while her corn-bread was frying, did not broil beautifully.

No, the temporary disappointment of Ni-ha-be and Rita was not the fault of Mother Dolores. Their mighty father was sitting where the odor of that cooking blew down upon him, and it made him hungry again before the steak was done. He called Red Wolf to help him, for the other braves were departing to their own camp-fires, and in a minute or so more there was little left of the supper intended for the two young squaws.

Dolores patiently cut and began to broil another slice, but that was Red Wolf's first supper, and it was the third slice which found its way into the lodge after all.

The strange part of it was that not even Ni-ha-be dreamed of complaining. It was according to custom.

There was plenty of time to eat supper after it came, for Dolores was compelled to look out for her own. She would not have allowed any other squaw to cook for her any more than she herself would have condescended to fry a cake for any one below the rank of her own husband and his family. Mere common braves and their squaws could take care of themselves, and it was of small consequence to Dolores whether they had anything to eat or not. There is more "aristocracy" among the wild red men than anywhere else, and they have plenty of white imitators who should know better.

William O. Stoddard

CHAPTER IX

There had been a very good reason why neither Steve Harrison nor Murray came back with the Lipan braves who were sent to bring home the game. They had been preparing to do so when they were summoned into the presence of To-la-go-to-de.

"No Tongue is a great hunter," said the dark-browed leader, as they came forward. "Cougar, big-horn, deer, all good. Apache heap better."

"That's what I came for."

"Go find them. Eat a heap. Take Yellow Head. Go all night."

"Any warriors go with me?"

"No. Maybe Apache dog see you. See pale-faces and not think of Lipans. Dress Yellow Head. Wash off paint."

It was a genuine stroke of Indian war cunning. The two pale-faces were to act as scouts in the advance. If the Apaches should happen to see them their presence would not suggest the dangerous nearness of a band of hostile Indians.

It may be the wise old chief added, to himself, that if both of them were killed on their perilous errand, the loss to his tribe would be of less consequence than that of two full-blooded Lipans. His pride of race would prevent his admitting that he had no brave in his band who was as well fitted to follow and find Apaches as was No Tongue.

"Now, Steve, we must eat all we know how, and then I'll fix you."

It had not harmed the young hunter in the opinion of his red friends that he had been unable to conceal his delight at the prospect before him.

"Young brave," they said, with approving nods. "Glad all over. Make good warrior some day."

He was indeed "glad all over," but Murray cautioned him by a look, and he said nothing.

He was almost too glad to eat, but his appetite came back to him while he and Murray were cooking. He had eaten nothing since morning, and mountain air is a very hungry sort of air.

"That's right, my boy. There's no saying when you may get your next square meal. There's hard work before you and me, and plenty of it."

The next thing that came to Steve was a surprise.

Murray had never worn paint or adopted any more of Indian ways than he could help, but it was a wonder how soon he made himself look like a white man.

There was more in the pack on his spare pony than Steve had imagined.

William O. Stoddard

A few minutes' work with a pair of small scissors made a remarkable change in his hair and beard, and then the long locks of Yellow Head himself had to suffer.

"Go and scrub off every spot of paint, while I'm rigging my hunting-shirt and leggings. You won't know me when you come back."

That was saying a little too much, but To-la-go-to-de himself expressed his admiration. He had seen wilder looking white men, by the hundred, among the border-settlements. No eyes in the world would suspect No Tongue of being a Lipan.

The transformation in Steve's appearance was shortly even greater, for Murray was able to furnish him with a "check" shirt and black silk neckerchief.

"Buckskin trousers'll have to do, my boy. No boots in camp, but I can knock the wrinkles out of this head-piece for you."

It was a black felt hat, and not very badly worn. Murray himself always wore one, but the supply had not been good enough for a long time to allow Steve to do the same.

"Now, Steve, I'm going to make old Two Knives give you the best mount in camp—good as mine."

Such a war-party never carries any slow horses with it, but there were some better than others, and the chief was as anxious as Steve that his "scouts" should be well mounted. Otherwise they might not be able to get back to him with any information they might pick up.

"Plenty of ammunition, Steve. Never mind any other kind of baggage, except some jerked meat. We may have to live on that."

There was no need for To-la-go-to-de to urge them. Not a minute was thrown away in their rapid preparations, and then the whole band turned out to see them ride away.

"I tell you what, Steve," said Murray, "we're not dressed in the latest fashion, but I haven't felt so much like a white man for years. I'll act like one, too."

There was a flash of pain in his eyes as he said that. Could it be he had ever done anything unworthy of his race and training?

Perhaps, for he had ridden on a great many warpaths with the fierce and merciless Lipans.

The latter would not follow till morning, and would move less rapidly than their two scouts, but their progress was not likely to be at all slow.

Steve Harrison rode on by the side of his friend for some distance without saying a word.

"What's the matter, Steve?"

"Murray, I don't mean ever to go back to the Lipans."

"Not unless it's necessary."

"It won't be necessary."

"Can't say, Steve. All this country's full of Apaches. We may get a sight of 'em any minute. I don't much care how soon we do, either."

"I'm not Indian enough for some things, Murray."

"Couldn't you fight Apaches?"

"I suppose I could, if they came to fight me. But I don't want to kill anybody. I thought you said you were feeling more like a white man."

"Steve, I don't know how I'd feel if I had a white shirt on, and a suit of civilized clothes. I'm a good deal of a savage yet, as it is."

"I never saw anything very savage about you."

"I'm on the war-path now, Steve, after my old enemies. Let's make as good time as we can before dark. After that we'll have to go carefully till the moon's up."

They were advancing a good deal more rapidly than the Apaches had been able to do over that same pass, hindered by their long train of tired pack-ponies and their women and children.

It was not a difficult trail to follow, for the lodge pole ends, dragging on the ground, had so deeply marked it that a man like Murray could have found it in the dark.

That was precisely what he did, after the sun sunk behind the western mountains, and the deep shadows crept up from the ravines and covered everything.

After the moon arose it was easier work, and Steve thought he had never seen anything more beautiful than was the moonlight on the quartz cliffs, and the forests, and the little lakes in the deep valleys, and on the foaming streams which came tumbling down the mountain sides from the regions of perpetual snow above.

Perhaps he was right, for hardly anybody has ever seen anything more beautiful in its way than such a moonlight view as that.

There was no time to stop and gaze, for Murray pushed on as fast as possible without using up their tough and wiry mustangs.

"We may need all the legs they've got to-morrow, Steve. We must find grass and water for them before daybreak."

It was a good three hours before sunrise, and the moon had again left them in darkness, when they almost groped their way down a steep declivity into a small hollow.

"Can't say how much there is of it, Steve, but this'll do. The Apache ponies have been cropping this very grass within twenty-four hours. Look at that."

"I can't see it very well."

"Feel of it, then. Don't you understand such a sign as that?"

"It's only a tuft of grass."

"Yes, but I found it ready pulled off, and it hasn't had time to more than wilt a little. The man that pulled it was here yesterday."

Murray did not know it, but no man had pulled that grass. It was a bunch Ni-ha-be had gathered for her pony, and then had thrown at Rita. Still, the guess about the time of it was nearly right, and that was a good enough place to rest in until daylight.

"No cooking this morning, I suppose," remarked Steve, when

Murray shook him out of the nice nap he had snatched, wrapped in his "serape," or Mexican blanket. "No breakfast, eh?"

"You don't know what tales a smoke might tell, or to whom it might tell 'em. Cold meat'll have to do for this time, and glad to get it. After that, Steve, you'll do the most dangerous riding ever you did."

"Why, are they so near?"

"Can't be many miles. Our first hunt, though, will be for a place to hide our horses in."

"Why not leave 'em here?"

"I thought of that, but we may need 'em."

Their morning ride was a longer one than Murray imagined, but before noon he was able to say,

"The backbone of the pass is miles behind us, Steve. All the rest of the way'll be down hill, or kind of up and down."

"Up and down" it was, but they had barely advanced another half-mile before Steve exclaimed,

"There they are, Murray!"

"There they are! What a valley it is, too! But, Steve, they don't mean to stay there."

"A spy-glass? I didn't know you had one! How do you tell that they won't stay?"

"The glass? It's a double one. Some army officer owned it

once, I suppose. I got it of old Two Knives himself. Nobody knows how it came to him. Look through it."

Steve had seen such things before, but had known very little about them. He did not even know how very good a glass that was with which he was now peering down upon the camp of the Apaches.

"See the lodge-poles lying there—in a dozen places?"

"They've put up some lodges."

"If they meant to stay they'd put up the others. No use for us to go back. The Lipans are coming along fast enough so long as the Apaches are on the move."

"But how can we get any farther? We can't ride right through them."

"I should say not; nor over them either. But if we can get into that pine-forest over there on the north slope, without being seen, we can ride around them."

"I'll risk it, Murray."

"So will I, Steve. I'd never let you try a thing like that alone."

"I could do it."

"Perhaps. And you'll have a good many things of that kind to do before you reach the settlements; but I guess I'll go with you this time."

"You'd better go with me all the way."

Murray said nothing, but he sprung from his horse, and Steve imitated him.

Men on foot were not so likely to be seen from the Apache camp.

There was nothing in or about that camp which Murray did not carefully study through his glass, and it showed him what was going on more clearly and perfectly than even the wonderfully keen black eyes of Ni-ha-be had shown it all to her, from almost the same spot, the day before.

"It's a hunting-camp, Steve, but it's a very strong party."

"Too strong for our Lipans?"

"I don't know about that. If we could surprise them by night we might do something with them."

"I'm no Lipan, Murray. None of those people down there ever did me any harm. Did they ever do you any? I don't mean any other Apaches; I'm just speaking of that camp."

"Well, no, I'm not sure about that. I don't know that I've any special grudge against this lot."

"Seems to me it's a good deal like an Indian to kill one man for what another man did. I'm only a boy, and I've been among the Lipans three years, but I've made up my mind to stay white."

Steve spoke with a good deal of energy, and his robust form seemed to stand up straighter.

"You're right, Steve; don't you do a thing that isn't fit for your color. I won't say anything more about myself just now."

If anybody had been listening to those two that morning, or indeed at any other time, he might have noticed something curious about the way Steve Harrison talked. It was not to be wondered at that a veteran like Murray should be slow of speech, and it suited well with his white hair and his wrinkles.

There was a good reason for it. Except when talking with Murray, Steve had not heard a word of English for three years.

Yes, there had been one other exception. When, ever he had found himself all alone he had talked to himself, asking and answering questions, and listening to his own pronunciation of the words.

"I shall get among white men some day," he thought, "and it would be a dreadful thing to be white myself and not talk white. Anyhow, I've learned Mexican Spanish since I've been out here, and I'll be glad enough to forget all I know of Indian talk."

He did not know it, but some things he said sounded ten years older and wiser just for his manner of saying them. Besides, he had had to think a great deal, and to keep most of his thoughts to himself. Not a great many boys do that.

"Come on, Steve. That ledge isn't badly broken. Horses can follow it, and it heads away right into the pine-forest. We must try it."

"We can get almost down into the valley without being seen."

"Yes, and we can find out if any good gap opens out of the valley to the northward."

CHAPTER X

Captain Skinner and his miners were quickly at the head of that ravine again, but the gold ledge stopped them all as if it had been a high fence.

"Cap," said the man called Bill, "of course them two fellers lit onto this mine. They couldn't ha' helped it. But they haven't done a stroke of work on it. Reckon we kin set up marks of our own."

"'Twont pay."

"We can't leave a claim like this."

Every man of the party was of the same opinion, and Captain Skinner said,

"Go ahead, boys. Only I can tell you one thing. We're going to move out of this, through that western gap, before daylight to-morrow morning. We're too near those red-skins down there to suit me. There's no telling how many there may be of them."

The men sprung to their work with a will. The first thing they did was to set up a "discovery monument" right in the middle of the ledge, at the head of the chasm.

Large flat stones were laid down, others carefully set upon them, and so up and up, till a pretty well shaped, four-sided pyramid had been made, six feet square and as many high.

Then two more, nearly as large, were set up at the ends of the ledge, where the gold vein disappeared in the high cliffs.

Seven strong men can do a great deal in a short time when they are in a hurry and all understand exactly what to do.

"Now we'll go for supper, and send out the rest."

"Must have a shaft begun and a blast fired."

The miners have a law of their own among themselves that a man who finds a mine must do some work on it and set up "marks," or else his claim to it is of no value.

These miners only paid no attention to another "law," that a man like Steve Harrison, for instance, is entitled to all the time required to do his work and set up his monuments. One part of the law is just as good as another.

The return to camp was quickly made, and there was news to tell all around, for the hunters not only brought in game but also the information that they "reckoned an army train could be hauled down that gap to the westward. It's almost as good as a road."

"We'll try it to-morrow," said the Captain.

He went out with all the men he could spare from camp as soon as supper was eaten, and they carried with them pickaxes, crow-bars, mining drills, and shovels. All the tools were pretty well worn, but they would answer for the work in hand.

William O. Stoddard

It was getting dark when they reached the ledge; but that was of less consequence after two huge bonfires had been built near the central monument, and heaped with fragments of fallen pine-trees. Then the work began.

"Gangs of three," said Captain Skinner—"one on each side. We'll have two shafts started. Bill, drill your blast right there."

The shafts would not have been needed for a long time in actually working out ore from a ledge like that, but two such holes would make a very deep mark that could not be wiped out, and the "blast" would make another.

It was hard work, but as fast as the men who were prying and picking loosened a piece of quartz, it was lifted away by their comrades, and it was a wonder how those two shafts did go down.

All the while Bill was tapping away with his hammer and drill on the spot pointed out to him, and was making a hole in the rock about the size of a gun-barrel.

"Two feet, Cap," he shouted at last. "That's as far as I can go with this drill, and it's the longest there is in camp."

"That'll do. Charge it. Our job's 'most done."

The night was cool, but the miners had kept themselves warm enough. They were not sorry to quit when their hard-faced little Captain ordered them out of the two holes; but it was odd to see such great, brawny fellows obeying in that way a man who looked almost like a dwarf beside them.

"Got her charged, Bill?"

"All right, Cap."

"Stand back, boys. Touch yer fuse, Bill."

That was a slow-match that stuck out of the hole he had drilled in the rock, and it led down to the charge of powder he had skilfully rammed in at the bottom.

"We can hardly afford to waste so much powder," the Captain had muttered, "but it won't do for me to cross 'em too much on such a thing."

Back they went for a hundred yards, while the fuse burnt its slow, sputtering way down through the "tamping" Bill had rammed around it.

They had not long to wait. The blazing fires lit up the whole ledge and the bordering cliffs, and the miners could see distinctly everything that happened on it. Suddenly there came a puff of smoke from the drill-hole. Then the rock outside of it, toward the chasm, rose a little, and a great fragment of it tumbled over down the ledge, while a dull, thunderous burst of sound startled the silence of the night, and awaked all the echoes of the cliffs and the canyon.

No such sound had ever before been heard there, by night or by day, since the world was made; but Captain Skinner and his miners were not thinking of things like that.

"That'll do, boys," he said. "There'll be powder-marks on that rock for twenty years. Our claim's good now, if any of us ever come back to make it."

The men thought of how rich a mine it was, and each one promised himself that he would come back, whether the rest did or not.

It is not easy to tire out fellows as tough as they were, but Captain Skinner was a "fair boss," as they all knew, and the men who stood sentinel around his camp that night were not the men who toiled so hard on the mine.

"He doesn't seem to need any sleep himself," remarked one of them to Bill, as they were routed out of their blankets an hour before daylight the next morning.

"You'll have to eat your breakfast on horseback, you three," he said to them. "Strike right for the gap, and if you come across anything that doesn't look right, you can send one of you back to let me know. Sharp, now! We won't be long in following."

Their horses were quickly saddled, and away they rode, each man doing his best, as he went, with a huge piece of cold roast venison. The Captain had remarked to them, "That'll do ye. Your coffee'll be just as hot as ours."

That meant that the cold water of one mountain stream was just about as pleasant to drink as that of another.

Bill and his two comrades were not the men to grumble over a piece of necessary duty like that, and they knew it was "their turn."

The sun was well up before they reached the head of the gap, and a glance showed them that it was all the hunters had prophesied of it. It was, in fact, a sort of natural highway from that table-land down to the valleys and plains of Arizona.

"This'll do first-rate," said Bill: "only I'd like to know what thar is at the lower eend of it."

"That's what we're gwine to look for. If ever we come back to work that mine, Bill, what ranches we can lay out on that level beyond the ruins!"

"Best kind. Raise 'most anything up thar."

No doubt of it; but now for some hours their minds and eyes were busier with the pass before them than with either mines or farming.

"Not a sign yet, Bill, and we're getting well down. See them pines?"

"Off to the left? Hullo! Put for the pines, boys! We'll nab those two! See 'em?"

"Coming right along up. All we've got to do is to 'bush our horses, and let 'em git past us."

"Only two squaws."

The three miners dashed on a minute or so till they could turn aside among the thick-growing cover of the forest.

They rode in a little distance, till they were sure they could not be seen from the pass; then they dismounted, tethered their horses, and slipped cautiously back to crouch among some dense bushes among the rocks within a few yards of the path by which any one coming up the gap must needs ride.

"We'll get 'em."

"Learn all we want to."

"Hullo, Bill, I can see 'em. That ain't all; thar's some kind of

William O. Stoddard

a brave not fur behind 'em."

"I see. Only one. Well, we kin take him too."

"Take him! Bah! knock him on the head. I don't exactly like to fire a gun just here."

"Old Skinner'd kill ye if ye gave that kind of warnin' to a crowd of redskins."

"Mebbe there isn't any."

"You don't know. Safe not to make too much noise, anyhow."

They might have fired every cartridge they had and not been heard by the Apaches in the valley; but there was no one to tell them so. At the same time they felt perfectly safe to talk, for they were sure there were no human ears near enough to hear them—so sure that they talked aloud and recklessly.

Perhaps it would have been as well for them to have imitated Captain Skinner, who hardly ever talked at all.

As it was, they had nothing to do but to wait, for their intended captives were evidently in no sort of hurry, and were laughing merrily as they loitered along the ravine below, picking berries here and a flower there, and making a capital frolic of their morning ride.

Laughing, talking, thoughtless of all danger, and yet they were riding on into the most terrible kind of a "trap."

How could any help reach them, if once they should go beyond those treacherous rocks and bushes?

CHAPTER XI

In such a country as that, full of sudden changes from mountain and table-land to valleys and plains, pretty large bodies of men might have been quite near each other without knowing it. Unless, indeed, they should send out sharp-eyed scouts to find out about their neighbors, as did the miners under Captain Skinner, and the Lipans of To-la-go-to-de.

Neither of these "main bodies" remained in camp an hour longer than was necessary, but even after they left their respective camps they moved onward with some caution, half expecting at any moment to see one of their scouts come riding back with important news.

The white men had heavy wagons to prevent them from moving rapidly, but their road toward the "western gap," and even through it, would be almost a straight line compared to the long, rugged, round-about pass over which Murray and Steve Harrison had followed the trail of the Apaches.

"Motion" was decidedly the order of the day, even for the Apaches. To be sure, there had been no known reason why they should bestir themselves so early in the morning; but their chief himself had given orders the night before, right after supper, that no more lodges should be set up, and that all things should be in condition for a march.

William O. Stoddard

He needed yet to make up his mind precisely in what direction the march should be, and Rita's "talking leaves" had not given him a single hint about that.

The fact that they had not was a trouble to him, but it was a little too much to expect of a chief and warrior that he should seem to go for counsel to a mere squaw, and a very young one—a squaw of the pale-faces at that. So Rita and Ni-ha-be had not been molested in their lodge all the evening, and a grand talk they had of it all by themselves, with Mother Dolores to listen.

Dolores had listened, but the girls had been surprised by the fact that she asked almost no questions at all—not even about the cavalry pictures.

She did not explain to them that her mind was all the while too completely filled with the thought of the one picture which had spoken to her, and made her shut her eyes and kneel down. There could not possibly be any other which could do more than that, although it was a great thing that Many Bears should have given them any attention.

Ni-ha-be had slept as soundly as usual that night, and Rita had "made believe" do so, until her adopted sister ceased even to whisper to her, and she could hear the loud breathing of Mother Dolores on the opposite side of the lodge.

Then she opened her eyes in the darkness, and tried to recall all she had seen in the three marvellous magazines, page by page.

How it all did come back to her! Some of the words, too, that she had not understood begun to have a meaning to her.

"They are talking now," she said to herself. "They are almost all talking. They are helping me remember. I'm sure that was my mother—my white mother. But where is my white father? He was not there at all. I must look for him again tomorrow. We must ride off away from the camp, where nobody can see us, and we can talk as much as we please."

"We" meant herself and Ni-ha-be, of course, but it also meant her three prizes. She had brought them to bed with her on her soft buffalo-skin, and she was hugging them closely now. It seemed to her as if they were alive, and had come to tell her almost anything she could think to ask.

Then it was all so still, and she was so tired with her journey and her excitement, that she fell asleep at last, to dream of more people and stranger things than had ever come to her mind before, sleeping or waking.

When morning came there was no need for Rita to propose a ride on horseback. Ni-ha-be spoke of it first, and for the self-same reason; but there was nothing unusual about it, for they almost lived in the saddle, like genuine daughters of the great Apache nation.

That, too, was why nobody paid them any attention when, an hour or so after their late breakfast, they were seen to scold a couple of wild-looking boys into bringing up their horses for them. The chief's two favorites were entitled to that much of service, and were apt to insist upon it.

For a while the very delight of galloping up and down the valley on such swift and beautiful animals as they were riding almost drove out of their minds the thought of talking leaves; but when, a little later, Many Bears slowly arose from a long fit of thinking, there in front of his lodge, and said to Red Wolf, "Call Rita," Rita was nowhere to be seen.

William O. Stoddard

"Find her. Tell her to come and bring me the white men's medicine, talking leaves."

Red Wolf sprang upon the nearest horse—and there were several standing ready for sudden errands—and dashed away in search of his truant sisters.

Mother Dolores could tell him nothing, but his loud, half-angry questionings drew together a knot of squaws and children, two or three of whom were ready to point toward the north-eastern slope of the valley, where it crept up through the pine-forest into the mountains, and tell him he would have to hunt in that direction.

He was ready for it, of course; but he reined in his mustang in front of his father long enough to tell him the cause of the delay.

"Bring them back. They are as wild as rabbits. They will lose their scalps some day."

The chief did not smile when he said that. He was beginning to feel uneasy about the position of his affairs, and he could hardly have told why. He said to himself, "Bad medicine. Can't see him. Great chief smell him."

And then he gave sharp orders to his young braves to have all the ponies caught and brought in from the pastures below, and to the squaws to have all their packs ready and their lodges taken down.

"Big talk come," he said again to himself. "Maybe big fight. Don't know. Must be ready. Somebody catch the great chief asleep if he doesn't look out."

Nobody had ever done that yet, for Many Bears had even a

greater name for his cunning than for his fighting.

Red Wolf was well mounted, and he darted away at full speed. His father was not a man to forgive a slow messenger any more than a slow cook.

"I understand," he muttered. "Squaws not stay in valley. Go among trees and rocks. Bears catch 'em some day. Eat 'em all up. Not afraid of anything."

So he was really anxious about them, and afraid they would run into danger?

Certainly.

The red man's family affection does not always show itself in the same way with ours, but there is plenty of it. All the more in the case of a young brave like Red Wolf, with every reason to be proud as well as fond of his sister.

And of Rita?

He was thinking of her now, and wondering if she had learned anything more about the cavalry from her talking leaves.

It was, for all the world, just as if he had been a young white man from "one of the first families." He galloped onward, keenly eying the fringes of the forest and the broken bases of the ledges, until he came to the broad opening below the gap, and here he suddenly stopped and sprung to the ground at a place where the green sod was soft and deeply marked with the prints of horses' hoofs.

"The blue-coat horsemen came out into the valley here. Their tracks are old. Ugh! Those are fresh. Ni-ha-be and Rita."

He was on his horse again in an instant, galloping up the not very steep slope of the pass.

The two girls had been in no hurry, and it was not long before Red Wolf came in sight of them.

He put his hand to his mouth and gave a long, peculiar whoop that meant: "I am after you. Come back!"

They understood it well enough, and Rita might have obeyed at once if she had been left to herself; but there was more than a little mischief behind the black eyes of Ni-ha-be.

"Let him catch us. He won't do anything worse than scold. I'm not afraid of Red Wolf."

Rita was, just a little, but she rode on beside her sister without turning her head.

"We shall not read any out of the leaves this morning."

"Read? What is that?"

"Just the same as a warrior when he finds the trail of a deer. Just like the trail of the blue-coat cavalry. Father and the gray-heads read it."

"Is that the way the leaves talk to you? I guessed it was. It is all signs, like tracks in the mud."

Rita had used the only Apache word she could think of that came at all near to meaning what she wanted, but there was no word for "book," or for any kind of book.

Again they heard the shout of Red Wolf behind them. It was nearer now, and a little angry.

"He is coming, Ni-ha-be. Don't let us ride fast."

"He is saying ugly things. But we will laugh at him, and tell him he cannot whoop loud enough to be heard."

Red Wolf was proud of his powerful voice, and that would be a sure way to tease him.

"Rita! The great chief is angry! He calls for you!"

He was close upon them by this time, and they reined in their horses. Teasing Red Wolf was one thing, but disobeying Many Bears was quite another.

They had seen squaws beaten for smaller offences than that.

"We have done wrong, Ni-ha-be."

"Oh, not much. We can ride back as fast as our ponies can carry us. Turn and meet him."

It had been a very little bit of a "runaway" on the part of the two girls, but it threatened to have serious consequences.

There was no time even for Red Wolf to scold them before the consequences began to come.

They had ridden just to the end of the spot where the rocks and bushes at the roadside were so thick-set and made so perfect a cover for anybody hiding among them.

"Look, Red Wolf! look!"

"Oh, who are they? Enemies!"

The young brave pulled in his mustang so sharply that he

almost tumbled him over, and turned his head.

"Pale-faces! How came they here?"

He could hardly have been more astonished if one of the granite bowlders near him had stood up and said, "Good-morning." So far as he could have guessed, the nearest white man was many hundreds of miles away, and his nation was at peace with them for the time; but here were three of the hated race standing in the road to cut oft his retreat and that of his sisters.

Three tall, brawny, evil-looking pale-faces, with rifles in their hands, and the foremost of them was levelling his gun straight at Red Wolf, and shouting, "Surrender, you red-skinned coyote, or I'll put a pill into ye."

An Indian brave, like the son of Many Bears, might deem it an honor to be named after the large, dangerous "wolf" he had killed in single fight with only his knife, but to be called a coyote, a miserable prairie wolf, jackal, was a bitter insult, and that was what it was meant for. He had left his carbine in the camp, but his long lance was in his hand, and his knife and revolver were in his belt.

What could one young brave do against three such powerful and well-armed white men?

"Ni-ha-be!" exclaimed Rita.

"I am an Apache girl! I can fight! You are a pale-face!"

Rita was stung to her very heart by her sister's scornful reply, for she had also brought her bow and arrows. They never stirred from camp without them, and squaws were not permitted to carry firearms.

Ni-ha-be had an arrow already on the string, and Rita followed her example like a flash.

"Red Wolf is a warrior. He is not a coyote. He will show the pale-faces—"

Twang!

The sound of Ni-ha-be's bow-string cut Red Wolf's haughty reply in two in the middle, and it was well for the miner "Bill" that he was quick in dodging. As it was, he dropped his rifle, for there was an arrow through his right arm above the elbow, and Ni-ha-be was fitting another.

Twang!

But the man at whom Rita aimed her arrow was an old Indian fighter, and he parried it easily.

"Red Wolf, your pistol!"

"Boys," exclaimed Bill, "they're a lot of young wild-cats! We'll jest have to shoot. Pick on the redskin, quick, and knock over the two girls before they make a hole into ye."

The two parties were hardly twenty yards apart, and all this had happened in a few seconds; but just then Red Wolf was exclaiming,

"Two more!"

And Rita said, excitedly,

"Stop, Ni-ha-be! See! They are fighting other. These two are friends. Don't shoot!"

William O. Stoddard

CHAPTER XII

During one part of the journey Steve Harrison and Murray had found the ledge along the mountain side pretty rough travelling, but their horses were used to picking their way along bad roads, and after a while they succeeded in getting out on to the comparatively smooth slope of the pine-forest.

"Our only risk now is that we may meet some of their hunters up here after game. We'll push right on."

"I'll fight if it can't be helped, Murray, but I'd a good deal rather not meet anybody."

"Well, so had I. Our business, just now, is scouting, not killing."

"I'll scout all day," said Steve.

"We must find a hiding-place for the horses, and creep down into the valley on foot. I'll show you some new tricks to-day."

The trees were large and the forest open, and no proper place was found for the concealment of such large animals, until they made their way at last to the very edge of the pass, at the point where it left the rugged cliffs of the "gap" and entered the more gentle slope of the forest.

"This'll do, Steve. I could hide a company in here; and no one squad need know where the next one was lying."

That was true enough, but it was of more importance to them that day than any one would have expected.

They tethered their horses between two rocks, where the thickly woven vines overhead made almost a dark stable for them.

"Now, Steve, a good look up and down, and we're off."

Between them and what could be called "the road" were many yards of tangled growth, and before they had gotten through it Steve felt his arm gripped hard.

"Listen! Horses coming! Lie still."

A minute more and they were both willing to lie as still as mice, for that was the very cover chosen by Bill and his two comrades in which to wait for their intended prisoners.

They and their horses were hardly twenty feet from Steve and Murray, and every loud word they said was distinctly heard.

Moreover, Murray and his young friend were on higher ground, and they, too, could look down the pass, and see who was coming.

"Two young squaws," whispered Murray. "The foolish young things are coming right into the trap."

"Can't we help 'em?"

"They're Apache squaws, Steve."

"I don't care. I'm white!"

"So am I. Tell you what, Steve—Ha! I declare!"

"What's the matter, Murray?"

"One of 'em's white! Sure's you live. They sha'n't touch a hair of their heads!"

"White or red?" whispered Steve, and he was not speaking of the color of Ni-ha-be's hair or of Rita's.

The expression of Murray's face astonished Steve. It was ghastly white, under all its tan and sunburn, and the wrinkles seemed twice as deep as usual, while the fire in his sunken eyes was fairly blazing. It was likely to be a bad time for anybody to cross the temper of "No Tongue," and Steve felt that his own blood was getting a little warm.

"There's an Indian coming."

"Apache. After the squaws. Don't you hear his whoop? I suppose they'll shoot him first thing, but they won't send a bullet at the girls. They're a bad crowd. Worse than Apache Indians."

"I don't consider them white men."

"Not inside, they ain't. I'd rather be a Lipan!"

The two merry, laughing girls rode by, in happy ignorance of the danger that was lurking in the thicket, and Red Wolf galloped swiftly on to join them.

Then the three miners, with Bill at their head, sprung out of their cover.

"Look out, boys. Don't use your rifles. Thar must be plenty more within hearin'."

"We'll have to kill the brave."

"Of course. Git close to him, though. No noise. I'd like not to give him a chance to so much as whoop."

They never dreamed of looking behind to see if any one were following them out of the cover, but it would have been better for them to have done so.

"They've start enough now," growled Murray. "Come on, Steve. Step like a cat. We must take them unawares. Have your tie-up ready."

The buckskin thongs which hang from the belt or shoulder or knee of an Indian warrior are not all put there for ornament. They are for use in tying things, and they are terribly strong. No human hand can break one, and they are always there and ready, only needing to be cut off.

Steve's face was almost as pale as Murray's in his excitement. He had looked in the bright faces of the two "young squaws" as they rode by, and it seemed to him as if he could fight those three miners all alone.

They saw Red Wolf join his sisters; they heard the startled cries of Rita and Ni-ha-be, the demand for their surrender, and Red Wolf's reply.

"Now, Steve, quick! Do just as I tell you!"

Twang went Ni-ha-be's bow at that instant, and the man next to Bill was raising his rifle to fire, when his arms were suddenly seized by a grasp of iron and jerked behind him.

"Right at the elbows, Steve. Draw the loop hard. Quick!"

As the next of the miners turned in his tracks he was astonished by a blow between the eyes that laid him flat, and saw a powerful-looking old man, of his own race, levelling a carbine at him saying,

"Give it up, boys. Don't one of ye lift a hand."

Bill could not lift his, with the arrow in his arm. The man Steve had tied could not move his elbows. The man on the ground was ruefully looking into the barrel of Murray's rifle. Besides, here was Red Wolf, springing forward, with his lance in one hand and his revolver in the other, while Rita held his horse, and Ni-ha-be sat upon her own, with her second arrow on the string.

"We give it up," said Bill. "But what are you fellers up to? I see. You're the two miners, and you're down on us because we jumped your claim to that thar gold ledge."

"Wall, Bill," grumbled one of his comrades, "I don't blame 'em for that; but they needn't ha' took sides with redskins."

Red Wolf lowered his lance and stuck his pistol in his belt. "Your prisoners. Not mine," he said to Murray. "Glad to meet friend. Come in good time."

He spoke in Mexican Spanish, but Murray understood him, and so did the miners.

"Hear him, Bill! He knows them two fellers. That's why they

ain't afraid to prospect away down here."

He had made a bit of a mistake, but Murray answered, short and sharp,

"Young brave take friend's advice. Jump on horse. Take young squaws back to camp. Tell chief to ride hard. Kill pony. Get away fast."

"Who shall I tell him you are?"

"Say you don't know. Tell him I'm an enemy. Killed you. Killed young squaws. Going to kill him."

There was a sort of grim humor in Murray's face as he said that. Not only Red Wolf, but the two girls, understood it, and the latter would have given a good deal to be able to tell the "white head," as they called him, and his handsome young friend, how thankful they both were.

Steve had not said a word, but he was narrowly watching the three miners for any signs of an effort to get loose. He and Murray might have been able to upset the two unwounded men in a fair fight, but it was just as likely to be the other way.

"It's that other one, Steve. He's watching his chance. That's it. Draw it hard. Now he won't be cutting any capers."

The expression of the miner's eyes promised the unfriendliest kind of "capers" if he should ever get an opportunity to cut them.

"It's no use, boys," said Bill. "Mister, will you jest cut this arrer, close to my arm, so's I can pull it out?"

"I will in a minute. It's as good as a tie of deer-skin jest now. Watch 'em, Steve!"

He walked forward a few steps as he spoke, and looked long and hard into the face of Rita.

"Too bad! too bad! They'd better have killed her, like they did mine. It's awful to think of a white girl growing up to be a squaw. Ride for your camp, young man. I'll take care of these three."

"I will send out warriors to help you. You shall see them all burnt and cut to pieces."

"Oh, Rita!" whispered Ni-ha-be; "they ought to be burnt."

Rita was gazing at the face of old Murray, and did not say a word in reply.

"Come," said Red Wolf; "the great chief is waiting for us."

And then he added to Murray and Steve,

"The lodges of the Apaches are open to their friends. You will come?"

"Steve, you had better say yes. It may be a lift for you."

"I will come some day," said Steve, quickly. "I don't know when."

"The white head must come too. He has the heart of an Apache, and his hand is strong for his friends. We must go now."

He looked at the three miners for a moment, as if he disliked leaving them behind, and then he bounded upon his pony, and the two girls followed him swiftly down the pass.

"Was he not handsome, Rita?"

Ni-ha-be was thinking of Steve Harrison, but Rita replied,

"Oh, very handsome! His hair is white, and his face is wrinkled, but he is so good. He is a great warrior, too. The bad pale-face went down before him like a small boy."

"His hair is not white, it is brown as the hair of a young buffalo. His face is not wrinkled. He is a young brave. He will be a chief."

"Oh, that other one! I hardly looked at him. I hope they will come. I want to see them again."

Red Wolf rode too fast for them to say much, and he did not pause until he reached the very presence of Many Bears and his counsellors.

There were already signs, in all directions, that the camp was beginning to break up, as well as tokens of impatience on the face of the chief.

"Where go?" he said, angrily. "Why do young squaws ride away when they are wanted?"

Ni-ha-be was about to answer, but Red Wolf had his own story to tell first, and he sternly bade her to hold her tongue till he had made his report. It was eagerly listened to.

Pale-face enemies so near! Who could they be? White friends, too, ready to fight for them against other white men, and send them warning of danger! That was more remarkable yet.

A trusty chief and a dozen braves were instantly ordered to dash into the pass, bring back the three prisoners, and learn all they could of the "white head" and his young companion.

Perhaps Steve Harrison would hardly have felt proud of the names which was given him on the instant. The only feat the Apaches knew of his performing was the thorough manner in which, according to Red Wolf, he had tied up those two miners; and so for lack of any other name they spoke of him as the "Knotted Cord." It was not long before Murray himself was known in that council by a long word, terribly hard to pronounce for any but an Apache, but that might be translated "Send Warning." He had actually earned a "good name" among his old enemies.

Rita and Ni-ha-be were saved any farther scolding. There was no time for that now, and the chief was more than ever anxious to ask questions of the "talking leaves," now he was sure of the neighborhood of danger.

Rita was puzzled.

"Ask about the bad pale-faces. Who are they?"

She took her three magazines from the folds of her antelope-skin tunic with trembling hands, for she was dimly beginning to understand that they could not tell her of things which were to be. It seemed to her, in that moment, that she could not read or remember a single word of English.

The one she opened first was not one which contained the pictures of the cavalry; but Rita's face instantly brightened, and she handed it to her father. There were five or six pages, one after the other, each of which contained a picture, large or small, of men engaged in mining for gold among the Western sierras.

The chief gravely turned the leaves till he came to a sketch that drew from him a sharp and sullen "Ugh!"

He had hit it, and there could be no mistake.

There were the sturdy miners, with rifles instead of picks, making a gallant charge upon an attacking party of Indians.

"No need to talk. Great chief see for himself. No lie. I remember. Kill some of them. Rest got away. Now they come to strike the Apaches. Ugh!"

That was a "fancy sketch" by some Eastern artist; but it must have been nearly true to life when an Apache chief could say he had been one of the very crowd of Indians who were being shot at in the picture.

"That do now. Talk more by-and-by. Big fight come."

The part of that band which could not fight was hurried forward at the best speed that could be made, while Many Bears rapidly transformed his buffalo-hunters into "warriors." All that was needed was to give them a chance to paint themselves in sufficiently hideous manner for the "war-path," and deal out to them a double allowance of cartridges for their rifles.

When that was done they made a formidable-looking array, and the last chance of the Lipans or any other enemies for "surprising" them was gone.

Then they rode slowly on after their women and children, and the braves came back from the pass to report to Many Bears that Send Warning, Knotted Cord, and their three prisoners had gone no one could guess whither.

CHAPTER XIII

For a moment Murray and Steve stood looking after the retreating forms of Red Wolf and his sisters.

"I say," exclaimed Bill, "you're a pretty pair of white men! Do you mean to turn us three over to them Apaches?"

"Who are you, anyway? Tell me a straight story, and I'll make up my mind."

"Well, there's no use tryin' to cover our tracks, I s'pose. We belong to the outfit that set up thar own marks on your ledge thar, last night. It wasn't any more our blame than any of the rest."

Murray nodded to Steve, as much as to say, "Keep still. We're learning something. Let him talk." But he replied to Bill,

"There's too many of your crowd for us to tackle. Where are the rest of you?"

"All coming down this way. We was sent ahead to scout."

"So you thought you'd make your outfit safe by picking a quarrel with the Apaches."

"Now, stranger, you've got me thar. 'Twas a fool thing to do."

"Well, I'll tell you what we'll do. You three stand up and swear you bear no malice or ill-will to me and my mate, and you and your crowd'll do us no harm, and I'll let you go."

"How about the mine?"

"Never mind about the mine. If your Captain and the rest are as big fools as you three, there won't any of you come back to meddle with the mine. The Apaches'll look out for that. There'll be worse than they are behind you, too."

He was speaking of the Lipans, but Bill's face grew longer as he listened, and so did the faces of his two friends.

"You know about that, do ye?"

"I know enough to warn you."

"Well, all I kin say is, we've got that dust, bars, nuggets, and all, and we fit hard for it, and we're gwine to keep it."

"What can you do with it here?"

"Here? We're gwine to Mexico. It'll take a good while to spend a pile like that. It took the Chinese a year and a half to stack it up."

"Well, if you don't start back up the pass pretty soon, you won't have any chance. Do you think you can keep your word with us?"

"Reckon we kin, with white men like you. So'll all the rest, when we tell 'em it don't cover the mine. You take your own chances on that."

"We do."

"Then we've no ill-will about this little scrimmage. Mebbe you did us a good turn."

"You may say that. Tell your mates I warn 'em to let the Indians alone down here. There's too many of 'em."

"Tell you what, now, old man, there's something about you that ain't so bad, arter all."

That was the remark of the first miner Murray set loose, but the second added,

"You've got a hard fist of your own, though. My head rings yet."

"It'd ring worse if it had been cracked by an Apache war-club. You and your mates travel!"

They plunged into the thicket for their horses, and when they came out again Murray and Steve had disappeared.

"Gone, have they?" said Bill. "And we don't know any more about 'em than we did before. What'll Captain Skinner say?"

"What'll we say to him? That's what beats me. And to the boys? I don't keer to tell 'em we was whipped in a minute and tied up by an old man, a boy, two girl squaws, and a redskin."

"It don't tell well, that's a fact."

It was the truth, however, and the three miners rode away up the pass in a decidedly uncomfortable frame of mind.

Murray had beckoned Steve to follow him, and they had slipped away among the rocks and bushes, but not too far to see what became of the three miners.

"They might have kept their word, Steve, and they might not. We were at their mercy, standing out there. They could have shot us from the cover."

"Oh, they are white men—not Indians. They never would do such a thing as that!"

"Wouldn't they! Didn't you hear him confess that they were trying to steal your mine? And didn't he say they were robbers, running away with stolen gold? Murderers, too? That's the kind of white men that stir up nine-tenths of all the troubles with the Indians. Let alone the Apaches: that tribe never did keep a treaty."

"The one we saw to-day looked like a Lipan."

"So he did, and he stood right up for the girls. He's a brave fellow. And, Steve, one of those young squaws was no more an Indian than you or I be. It makes my heart sore and sick to think of it. A fine young girl like that, with such an awful life before her!"

"The other one was bright and pretty, too, and she can use her bow and arrows."

"Full-blooded Indian. As full of fight as a wild-cat, and twice as dangerous."

"Now, Murray, what do you think we'd better do?"

William O. Stoddard

"Do? I wish I could say. My head's all in a whirl somehow. I want a chance to do some thinking."

"Time enough for that."

"Not if we keep right on after the Apaches. I'll tell you what, Steve, my mind won't be easy till I've had another look at the ledge. I want to know what they've done."

"The Buckhorn Mine? I'd like to see it, too."

"Then we'll let their outfit go by us, and ride straight back to it. Might as well save time and follow those fellows up the pass. Plenty of hiding-places."

It was a bold thing to do, but they did it, and they were lying safely in a deep ravine that led out of the pass, a few hours later, when the "mining outfit" slowly trundled on its downward way.

Long before that, however, Bill and his two friends had made their report to Captain Skinner.

They had a well made up story to tell him, but it was not very easy for him to believe it.

"Met the two mining fellers, did ye? And they're friends with the 'Paches. Wouldn't let 'em do ye any harm. How many redskins was there?"

"Three. We never fired a shot at 'em nor struck a blow, but one of thar squaws fired an arrer through my arm."

"It's the onlikeliest yarn I ever listened to."

"Thar's the hole in my arm."

"Not that. It isn't queer an Apache wanted to shoot ye. I can believe that. But that you had sense enough not to fire first at a redskin. You never had so much before in all your life."

"Here we are, safe—all three."

"That's pretty good proof. If there'd been a fight they'd ha' been too much for you, with two white men like them to help. Well, we'll go right on down. It's our only show."

"That isn't all, Cap."

"What more is there?"

"The old fellow told me to warn you that thar was danger comin' behind us. He seems to know all about us and about what we did to the ledge."

"We're followed, are we? What did he say about the mine?"

"Said he'd take his chances about that. We agreed to be friends if we met him and his mate again."

"You did? Now, Bill, you've shown good-sense again. What's the matter with you to-day? I never heard of such a thing? It's like finding that mine just where I didn't expect to."

Bill's two associates said nothing. They were quite willing he should do the talking, so long as he did not tell how they had been knocked down and tied up. But one of them had to pucker up his mouth for a sort of silent whistle when he heard Captain Skinner praise them for their wisdom in keeping the peace with the Apaches.

Perhaps all three of them, too, were thinking of what they should say if the exact truth about that morning's work

William O. Stoddard

should ever leak out.

Danger behind them. They did not know exactly what, but their consciences told them what it ought to be. That made it grow bigger and bigger the longer they thought of it.

Danger before them in the shape of wandering Apaches; but they had expected to meet that sort of thing, and were ready for it. Only they hoped to dodge it in some way, and to get safely across the border into Mexico with their stolen treasure.

They had at least made sure of their wonderful mine, and that was something. Sooner or later they would all come back and claim it again, and dig fortunes out of it. The two miners would not be able to prove anything. There was no danger from them.

Perhaps not; and yet, as soon as they had fairly disappeared down the pass, below the spot where Steve and Murray were hiding, the latter exclaimed, "Now, Steve, we won't rest our horses till we get there."

They would be quite likely to need rest by that time, for the old man seemed to be in a tremendous hurry.

Steve would hardly have believed anything could excite the veteran to such a pitch, if it had not been that he felt so much of the "gold-fever" in his own veins. It seemed to him as if he were really thirsty for another look at that wonderful ledge.

They turned their horses out to feed on the sweet, fresh grass at last, and pushed forward on foot to the mine.

"They've done it, Steve!"

"I see they have. Our title's all gone!"

He spoke mournfully and angrily; but Murray replied,

"Gone? Why, my boy, those rascals have only been doing our work for us."

"For us? How's that?"

"It was ours. They've set up our monuments, and dug our shafts, and put in a blast for us. They haven't taken anything away from us. I'll show you."

He had taken from a pocket of his buckskins a small, narrow chisel as he spoke, and now he picked up a round stone to serve as a hammer.

"I'm going to make a record, Steve. I'll tell you what to do about it as I go along."

Captain Skinner's miners had been hard workers, but Steve had never seen anybody ply a chisel as Murray did. He was not trying to make pretty letters, but they were all deeply cut and clearly legible.

On the largest stone of the central monument, and on the side monuments, and then on the face of the cliff near the ledge, he cut the name of the mine, "The Buckhorn," and below that on the cliff and one monument he cut the date of discovery and Steve Harrison's name.

"Put on yours too, Murray."

"Well, if you say so. It may be safer. Only I turn all my rights over to you. I'll do it on paper if I ever get a chance."

"I only want my share."

All the while he was chiselling so skilfully and swiftly Murray was explaining to Steve how he was to act when he reached the settlements, and how he should make a legal record of his ownership of that property.

"You must be careful to describe all these marks exactly; the ruins, too, the canyon, the lay of the land, the points of the compass—everything. After all, it may be you'll never be able to work it. But you're young, and there's no telling. The first thing for you to do is to get out of the scrape you're in now."

Steve felt as if there were no longer any doubt of that.

During the busy hours spent on the ledge by their masters the two horses had been feeding and resting, and both Murray and Steve felt like following their example.

"Start a fire, Steve; it'll be perfectly safe. I'll try for a deer, and we'll cook enough to carry us for two days."

CHAPTER XIV

The advance of To-la-go-to-de and his Lipans that day had been a slow one. It grew slower and more cautious as hour after hour and mile after mile of rugged mountain riding went by without any word from the two pale-face scouts.

The chief himself grew uneasy, and he would have sent another party in search of No Tongue and the Yellow Head but for fear of defeating the very object he had in view.

They, he thought, would surely return or send him some word before nightfall; but the sun was nearly setting when at last he went into camp with his discontented warriors on the very spot where Steve and Murray had made their own halt before daylight.

Then, indeed, he could wait no longer, and several braves were ordered out on foot, with others on horseback, a little behind them, to explore what was left of the pass and see what they could find. They could have done more for their chief and themselves if the night had not been a somewhat cloudy one, and not a brave of them ventured to descend into the valley.

If they had done so they might have discovered two very important facts. The first was that the Apache hunting village had left it, bag and baggage, no one could guess whither. The second, and quite as important a discovery, would have been that the camping-ground abandoned by the Apaches had been promptly occupied by a strong party of pale-faces.

All the scouts could really do was to bring back word that the pass was clear of enemies to the border of the valley.

That was an anxious night, therefore, for To-la-go-to-de, and it would hardly have been less so if he had known all about the doings of No Tongue and Yellow Head during the day—about their capture and release of the three miners, and their return to their mine.

The morning would bring news, at all events, for To-la-go-to-de determined to dash on with all his warriors and find it for himself.

"No Tongue is wise. He is a great warrior. Sometimes wise old warrior gets knocked on the head. Then he not come back at all."

There was a possibility, as he well knew, that the Apaches themselves had something to do with the silence of his two pale-face friends; but the Lipan chief was not the man to lie awake over any such thing as that; he was not even anxious enough to dream about them after he got asleep.

Another head had been quite as busy and troubled as that of To-la-go-to-de all that day, and Captain Skinner also would have given something for a few minutes' conversation with "them two mining fellers."

He felt sure they could have given him both information and advice; but he said to himself, "Of course they won't come nigh our outfit. They know we've jumped their claim. Still, they did the friendly thing with Bill and the boys, and they sent word they didn't bear us any ill-will. That's 'cause they feel sure of their own ground. They're on good terms with the redskins. I wish I could say we were."

Well he might, considering how many of them there were in that country, and how near to him some of them were coming.

All the way down the pass the ragged little "Captain" had ridden in advance of his men, carefully scanning every rock, and bush, and tree. At last he paused at the very spot where Bill and his companions had had their little difficulty. He seemed to see some signs that needed studying, and he stooped down and picked up something—only a pair of strong thongs of buckskin, that looked as if they had been recently used in tying up something. He could make very little out of them; but he noticed the marks of horse's feet going up and out of the forest.

"Signs are getting pretty thick. Hullo! An arrow! Cut in two, and blood on it. Bill, isn't this the spot?"

"This 'ere's the very place, Cap. We came awful nigh havin' a fight right yer."

"Glad you made out not to have any. Did those two white men and the Indians ride away in company?"

"Wal, no. The redskins rid away first, and the two fellers promised to foller 'em after a while. Then I reckon they cut off into the timber. 'Peared like they must ha' been huntin'."

"Most likely they were; and waiting for us to get away, so they could go back to their mine. Boys, I'm afraid our claim there won't be worth a great deal by the time we get back."

"We'll take care of that when we come, Cap. They said they'd take thar chances. We'll jest take ours; that's all."

Slower, more and more cautiously, the mining train again moved forward, until, from under the last of the pine-trees, Captain Skinner could look out upon the valley and see that it was empty.

How would he and his men have felt if they could have known that at that very minute Murray was chipping away with his chisel at his inscriptions upon the central monument of the great Buckhorn Mine?

"Not a redskin in sight," he remarked. "If there were any there this morning they've moved on. They're always on the move. Glad of it. We'll go straight on down. There must be plenty of ways out of a valley like that."

No doubt of it; but the first business of those wanderers, after they reached the spring and unhitched their mule-teams, was to carefully examine every hoof-mark and foot-print they could find.

The fact that there had been lodges there was proof that the Apaches were not a war-party, but there was plenty of evidence that they were numerous enough to be dangerous.

"Glad Bill didn't pick a quarrel with such a band as that," grumbled Captain Skinner. "But how did he happen to show so much sense? I never suspected him of it."

That was not very complimentary to Bill, and it was evident that the Captain's opinion of him had not changed.

"Some kind of an accident," he said. "Nobody need waste any time looking out for another one just like it."

It was getting late in the day, and a better place for a camp could not have been found.

"This'll do for to-night, won't it, Cap?" asked one of the miners.

"Of course it will. We'll try to move east from here, or south, when we leave it."

"Shall any of the boys go for game? Must be plenty of it all around."

"Game? Oh yes; plenty of it, after a hundred Apache hunters have been riding it down for nobody knows how long! The redskins leave heaps of game behind 'em, always."

The bitter sarcasm of the Captain's answer prevented any farther remarks on the subject of hunting that afternoon. They had plenty of fresh meat with them, nevertheless, and there was no reason why they should not cook and eat.

There was a reason why they could not at once be altogether pleased with their camping-ground. It was because they found the ashes of one fire still hot enough to kindle with.

"The Apaches haven't been out of this a great while," said Captain Skinner; "but the trail of their lodge-poles when they went shows that they set off to the west'ard. That isn't our direction. I don't care how far they go nor how fast."

When he came to talk with the other miners he found that they hardly felt as he did about it; neither did they like the looks of the mountain range through which the Apaches had come.

"Danger behind us or not," said one of the men. "I move we

William O. Stoddard

spend a day or so in huntin', and findin' out jest what's best to be done, before we light out of this. We must be getting pretty close to the Mexican line."

They were even closer than he had any idea of; but, when their evening conference ended, Captain Skinner was outvoted, and a "hunt and scout" was agreed upon for the next day.

CHAPTER XV

Ni-ha-be and Rita had escaped any scolding from Many Bears; but when the story of their morning's adventure was related to Mother Dolores that plump and dignified person felt bound to make up for the chief's neglect. She scolded them in the longest and hardest words of the Apache language; and when she could not think of anything new to add she begun again, and said it all over in Mexican Spanish. By that time she was out of breath, and Ni-ha-be exclaimed,

"I don't care, Mother Dolores—I hit one of them in the arm with an arrow. It went right through. Rita missed; but she isn't an Apache."

"Two young squaws!" said Dolores, scornfully. "Where would you have been now, and Red Wolf too, if it wasn't for that old pale-face and his boy?"

"He wasn't his boy," said Rita. "He didn't look like him a bit."

"Didn't he? And what are all your talking leaves good for? Why didn't they tell you to stay in camp?"

"I didn't ask them. Besides, that isn't what they're good for."

"Not good for much, anyhow. I don't believe they can even cure the rheumatism."

Poor Dolores had never heard the story of the squaw who had a tract given her by a missionary, and who tied it on her sore foot, but that was a good deal her idea of some of the uses of printing.

"No," said Rita, "I don't believe they're good for rheumatism."

"Anyhow," said Ni-ha-be, "the whole camp is getting ready to move. Come, Rita, let's you and I ride on ahead."

"No you won't, not either of you. You'll stay near me now. If the great chief wants you again, I must have you where I can find you."

The girls looked at one another, but there was no wisdom in a rebellion. They had offended quite enough for one day.

"Ni-ha-be," said Rita, "we can keep close together. They won't go fast, and we can look at the leaves all the way."

On an ordinary march a good many of the squaws would have had to go on foot and carry their pappooses, and perhaps heavy loads besides; but the orders of Many Bears prevented that this time. The poorest brave in camp had a pony provided for his wife and children, and as many more as were needed for all his baggage, for the chief was in a hurry, and there was to be no straggling. His orders were to push on as fast as possible until the squad of braves who had ridden ahead should find a safe spot to camp in—one that could be more easily defended than the exposed level they were leaving.

The idea of coming danger, too, was going around among the squaws themselves, and they were in as great a hurry as Many Bears. They did not know exactly what to be afraid of, but they did not feel any better on that account, with such a swarm of little copper-colored children to take care of.

Some ponies had more to carry and some had less, but there was one poor little, long-eared, patient-looking mule who had more than his share. There was no saddle on him, but where a saddle might have been sat a very fat and dreadfully homely squaw, with a pappoose on her back, his round head popping out, as if all he wanted was to look at the country as they went along.

The squaw rode her mule after the fashion of her people, and that was just as if she had been a brave instead of a squaw. But no brave in all the band would have allowed a twelve-year-old boy to climb up in front of him, as she did, or let his younger brother and sister cling on behind her; so that the little mule was turned into a sort of four-footed omnibus.

It did seem, too, as if there were more and more wretched-looking dogs following after that forlorn mule than behind the ponies of any chief's family in the whole band.

"Look, Rita," said Ni-ha-be—"look at old Too Many Toes and her mule!"

That squaw had a name of her own, as well as anybody, but it had not been given her for her beauty.

"Isn't she homely?" said Rita. "I wonder where the rest of her children are?"

"I guess she's divided them around among her relations. There's enough of them to load another mule. Her husband'll never be rich enough to buy ponies. He's lazy."

"He doesn't beat her?"

"He's too lazy for that. And he's afraid of her. I don't believe he's an Apache. Think of a brave afraid of his own squaw!"

There was something very bad in that, according to all Indian notions; but Rita only said,

"What would that mule do if she wanted him to run?"

Just then the shrill voice of Mother Dolores behind them shouted,

"I'm coming. They wanted to make me help them pack!"

The pride of the best cook in the band was seriously offended. As if all such hard work did not properly belong to ugly and ignorant squaws who had not education enough to fry corn-bread for the great chief! She knew her dignity better than that, and she meant to assert it. Perhaps if Many Bears himself had been close at hand, Dolores might have been more willing to work, but there was no opportunity for any appeal to him, and she took her own way.

She was all the more willing that her two charges should ride on to the very head of the little column, and even keep away a short distance to the right of it. They were perfectly safe within whooping distance if they were wanted, and none of the other squaws of Many Bears would dare to leave their ponies and baggage to come and scold. That was worth something.

Silent and submissive as are all Indian women in the presence of braves or of white men, they make up for it all in the use they make of their tongues among themselves. They can talk wonderfully fast and say as many sharp things as may be necessary.

"Now, Rita, see if you can make the leaves tell you anything about Knotted Cord."

"He isn't in them; nor Send Warning either."

"Look. They must be there."

Neither Steve Harrison nor Murray were to be found in the pages of those three magazines; Rita felt sure of that; but she turned the pages carefully as she and Ni-ha-be rode on side by side at a very slow walk.

She came to something else, however, in the back part of one of them which almost drove from her mind the face and form of Send Warning. Ni-ha-be forgot the brown hair and handsome face of the Knotted Cord.

"Oh, so many squaws!"

"All of them so tall, too. I wonder if pale-face squaws ever grow as tall as that? Look at the things on their heads."

"See!" exclaimed Rita. "All clothes! No squaws in them."

"Great chief. Ever so many squaws. Lose part of them. Keep their blankets."

Rita could not quite explain the matter, but she knew better than that.

The series of pictures which so excited and puzzled the two Indian maidens was nothing in the world but what the

William O. Stoddard

publishers of that magazine called "A Fashion Plate Supplement."

There was enough there, indeed, to have puzzled anybody. Gradually they began to understand it a little, and their wonder grew accordingly.

"Are they not ugly?" said Ni-ha-be. "Think of being compelled to wear such things. I suppose, if they won't put them on, they get beaten. Ugh! All black things."

"No. Only black in the pictures. Many colors. It says so; 'red,' 'yellow'—all colors."

That was better, and Ni-ha-be could pity the poor white squaws a little less. Rita allowed her to take that magazine into her own keeping; but mile after mile went by, and all she found in it worth studying was that wonderful array of dresses, with and without occupants. She had never dreamed of such things before, and her bright young face grew almost troubled in its expression.

Oh, how she did long just then for a look at a real pale-face woman, gotten up and ornamented like one of those pictured on the pages before her! She was learning a great deal—more than she had any idea of.

But Rita had learned a great deal more; for the faces and the dresses had joined themselves in her mind with ever so many things that came floating up from her memory—things she had forgotten for so long a time that they would never have come back to her at all if something like this had not stirred them up.

Just now, while Ni-ha-be had the fashion plates, Rita was busy with the illustrations of "gold-mining" which had so aroused the mind of Many Bears.

Not that she knew or cared anything about mines or ores or miners, but that some of those pictures also seemed to her to have a familiar look.

"Did I ever see anything like that?" she murmured to herself. "The great chief says he did. It is not a lie. Maybe it will come back to me some day. I don't care for any more pictures now; I'll try and read some words."

That was harder work; but there were strange, new thoughts beginning to come to Rita.

"You have not spoken to me," said Dolores at last. "Do the leaves talk all the while?"

"Look at these," said Ni-ha-be. "They are better than the one you cut out. There's only one squaw in that, and a pappoose. Here are ever so many. And look at the funny little children. How those things must hurt them! The pale-faces are cruel to their families."

Dolores look earnestly enough at the fashion plates. With all her ignorance she had seen enough in her day to understand more of them than the girls could. Once, long ago, when the band of Many Bears had been near one of the frontier "military posts," where United States troops were encamped, she had seen the beautiful "white squaws" of the officers, in their wonderful dresses and ornaments, and she knew that some of these were much like them. She could even help Ni-ha-be to understand it.

Rita had been silent a very long time. All the while the train had travelled nearly five miles. Now she suddenly exclaimed, "Oh, Ni-ha-be! Dolores!" And when they turned to look at her her face was perfectly radiant with triumph and pleasure.

"What is it? Have you found either of them?"

"I can do it! I have done it!"

"What have you done?"

"It is a story talk. Big lie about it all, such as the Apache braves tell at the camp-fire when they are too lazy to hunt. I have read it all."

"Is it a good talk?"

"Let me tell it. I can say it all in Apache words."

That was not the easiest thing in the world to do. It would have been impossible, if the short story which Rita had found had not been of the simplest kind—only about hunters following chamois in the Alps and tumbling into snow-drifts, and being found and helped by great, wise, benevolent St. Bernard dogs.

There were mountains in sight of the girls now that helped make it real, and among them were big-horn antelopes as wild as the chamois, and with very much the same habits. There were snow-drifts up there, too, for they could see the white peaks glisten in the sinking sun. It was all better than the talk of the braves around the winter camp-fires; and, besides, there were the pictures of the dogs and of the chamois. Neither Ni-ha-be nor Dolores uttered a word until Rita had rapidly translated that "story talk" from beginning to end.

"Oh, Rita! are there any more talks like that?"

"Maybe. I don't know. Most of them are very long. Big words, too—more than I can hear."

"Let me see it."

The pictures of the great, shaggy dogs and of the chamois were easy enough to understand. Ni-ha-be knew that she could see a real "big-horn" at a greater distance than Rita. But how was it that not one word came to her of all the "story talk" Rita had translated from those little black "signs" on those two pages of the magazine? It was quite enough to try the patience of a daughter of a great chief, but Dolores said,

"Never mind, Ni-ha-be; if the talking leaves could speak Apache you and I could hear the stories and tell them to Rita?"

That was a little comforting, but Ni-ha-be knew there were no illustrated monthly magazines printed by any of her people, and she grew more and more jealous of her adopted sister.

"Anyhow," she said, "you must hear them all and tell them to us. If any of the words are too big for you, you can leave them out."

Perhaps she could have done that, but what would then have become of the stories and other things?

Rita's prizes promised to be a source of a good deal of annoyance to her, as well as pleasure and profit. They did one thing for all three that day—they made the afternoon's ride across the grassy rolls of the plain seem very short indeed.

Only a few warriors were to be seen when the order to halt was given; but they had picked out a capital place for a camp—a thick grove of large trees on the bank of a deep, swift river. There were many scattered rocks on one side of the grove, and it was just the spot Many Bears had wanted. It was what army officers would call "a very strong position, and easily defended."

CHAPTER XVI

Murray's hunt was a short one, for that grassy tableland, with its cool streams and its shady trees, seemed to be a favorite pasture-ground for the mountain-deer. It is not likely they were often annoyed by hunters of any kind, and they were comparatively easy to approach. Besides, it was not necessary for a marksman like Murray to get so very near.

"A fine fat doe," said Steve, when his friend threw down his game in front of the fire.

"Now for a cooking time," replied Murray; "and then we must have a good nap."

"I'll do a little eating, too, while I'm cooking."

Neither of them neglected that duty, but Murray took the two plump hind-quarters of the doe and roasted them whole. How?—with no stove, no oven, no kitchen tools of any sort or description?

Two forked sticks were set firmly in the ground on either side, in front of the fire, and a strong stick laid across from fork to fork at about four feet from the ground; then a leg of venison, hung to this cross-piece by a thong of raw deer-skin, was turned around and around until the thong would twist no tighter. When it was let go the weight of the meat kept it from untwisting too fast; but it turned around in the opposite direction for ever so long, and it was roasting all the while.

It was precisely what our own great-grandmothers used to call a "roasting-jack," and all it required was somebody to wind it up when it ran down, so that the meat could be evenly done all over.

Meantime the broiling and eating of smaller pieces went right on, and neither Steve nor his friend seemed to have lost their appetite by their long ride and hard work.

"Now, Steve, lie down. Sleep all you can."

"Sha'n't you take a rest?"

"Don't need much. Young eyes call for more sleep than old ones. Lie right down and never mind me. I'll call you when your time comes."

Steve was used to paying the old man a pretty good kind of obedience, and he was glad enough to obey him now. He was quickly asleep under a spreading tree, while Murray sat down before the fire, as if to "mind the roast." There was something more important than venison for him to think of, however. He had taken off his hat, and his white head was bare. With the strong light of the camp-fire shining upon his weather-beaten face he would have made a good subject for a painter. He was thinking deeply—so deeply that at last he thought aloud:

"I am a white man. I've been an Indian long enough. Yes, I think I'll try it. That would be better than killing all the Apaches between this and the California line."

He did not explain what it was he meant to try, or why it would be so much better than killing Apaches; but the stern expression on his face grew milder and milder, until it almost seemed as if he were smiling, and even Steve Harrison had never seen him do that.

The venison roasts were wound up, twisted tight again and again, and at last they were taken off.

"They'll do. I'll give 'em an hour to cool, and then we must be off. I'll pack the rest of the meat raw, but we haven't left much of it."

To much to throw away for men who were not sure of their regular meals, and were very sure of getting hungry.

The hour went by, and then Steve felt himself rudely shaken by the shoulder.

"You can't have it," grumbled Steve. "That gold's ours. I killed it myself, and we're roasting it now."

"Dreaming, are you? Wake up, Steve; it's time we were moving. We've a long night ride before us."

"How late is it?"

"No watch. Can't say exactly; but I reckon we can reach the valley by sunrise, and not overwork our horses. They're both in good condition."

The great heavy carriage and road horses used in the "settlements" would not have been in anything like as good condition as were those two wiry, tough, swift-footed mustangs, after all they had been through. They were ready now for another long pull; but they were likely to stand it

William O. Stoddard

better in the cool night hours than under the hot sun.

In a few minutes more the two friends were in the saddle. There was no more that they could do just then for the safety of the Buckhorn Mine; but they had not ridden far before Murray suddenly exclaimed,

"I'm going to do a queer thing, Steve Harrison!"

"You won't go back to the Lipans?"

"Queerer than that. I'm going to ride straight in among that band of Apaches!"

"What for?"

"I can't exactly say as yet. Will you go with me?"

"Anywhere. I'll feel safer about not getting into the hands of the Lipans again."

"They never did you any hurt."

"I should say they did. It's hurt enough to stay among them for three long years."

"Think of what you've learned by it, my boy. And now you've found a gold-mine."

"And it isn't worth ten cents to me. Nobody'd give me a new hat for it."

"You will need one by the time you get to the settlements. We must try and look out for that. The main thing for us to-night is to see that we don't get into bad company."

"Either Lipans or miners. I believe one is about as bad as the other."

They had plenty to talk about but some parts of the pass they were following were densely dark, and they had to feel their way a foot at a time like a pair of blind men. It was slower work than riding over the same ground by day, and Murray turned out nearly right in his calculation of the time they would reach the valley. It was just as the light of the rising sun grew strong and bright that he and Steve stood on the slope at the lower edge of the forest, taking turns at looking through the spy-glass at the white tilts of the two wagons of the miners.

"They've roused up early for something," said Murray.

"Looks as if they were setting out on a hunt or a scout."

"So it does. There they go. Steve, we must ride after those fellows."

"What for?"

"To stop 'em. They'll only run their heads against the Apaches, and leave their camp to be plundered by the Lipans."

"They're in a trap, Murray."

"Come on, Steve!"

But the distance was not less than a couple of miles, and the miners had prepared beforehand for that "early start." It was all against the will of Captain Skinner, and the bad temper he was in only made him start more promptly, and ride faster.

"Tell ye what, boys," he said to the rest, as they galloped on behind him, "I'll give ye all the scouting you want this morning."

At that very moment Murray was saying, "No, Steve, we won't waste any time going to the camp. There's only three men left there. We must catch those fellows and send them back. What are they going so fast for? Why, it'll be a regular race!"

It was very much like one after a little. True, Steve and Murray were riding a good deal more rapidly than the miners; but it takes a great deal of swift running to catch up with men who have more than two miles the start of you, even if you travel two miles to their one, and the "chasers" in this case were not doing nearly so much as that.

"We'll catch 'em, Murray."

"If we don't it'll be a bad race for them. I kind o' feel as if the lives of those men were the prize we're riding for. We mustn't let our horses get blown. If we do, it's good-bye to that crowd ahead of us."

Mile after mile went by, and the excitement of it grew to be something terrible.

"The Apaches can't be far ahead of 'em now, Murray."

"Hark! Hear that?"

"A rifle shot—a whoop!"

"They are pulling up."

"They'd better. I'm afraid we're too late, Murray."

"On, on, Steve! Maybe there's time yet."

Captain Skinner had already seen and heard enough to make him halt his men, and he was gathering them rapidly into close order, when a long, ringing shout behind him drew his anxious eyes from the dangerous-looking "signs" now gathering in his front.

Signs? Yes, danger signs. Wild, dark, painted horsemen riding hither and thither and nearer and nearer, growing more and more numerous every moment. Those were the signs that Many Bears and his warriors meant to stand between any approaching enemy and the camp of their squaws and children. That was a quite a distance yet, but the Apaches did not mean to let any peril come very near it.

The shout was from Murray.

"Don't shoot!"

And in a few seconds more the old man was reining in his panting mustang among the startled and gloomy-faced miners.

"Where did you drop from?" was the cool, steady question of Skinner.

"Never you mind. Is Bill here?"

"He and his two mates are on guard at the camp. I know ye now; you're them two mining fellers. You met Bill and—"

"Yes, I met Bill; but there's no time for talk now. You take your men straight back to camp. It's the only show you've got left."

"Reckon we can beat off a few beggarly Apaches."

"Don't talk. Ride for your camp. If you get there before the Lipans do, take your wagons into the pass, and stay there till they get by. Don't strike a blow at them; they'd be too much for ye."

"Lipans? Going for our camp? Boys, 'bout face! Ride for your lives!"

For so small a man he had a great deal of voice, and his command was instantly obeyed; but he paused long enough to ask of Steve and Murray, "What about you two?"

"Us? We'll stay and keep the Apaches from chasing you."

"Won't they scalp you?"

"Not a bit. But there's one thing you may do. If by any chance you have a talk with the Lipans, you may tell them just where you saw us last. Tell the chief for me that No Tongue and Yellow Head are all right, only their horses are tired, following your trail and the Apaches."

"Hope I won't meet him! You're the queerest pair I ever saw. But I wish the boys had let me foller out the word you sent in by Bill."

"Too late now. Ride out of this the best gait your horse knows."

That too was good advice, and Captain Skinner took it; while the old man sat quietly in his saddle, with Steve Harrison at his side, as if they two were quite enough to stem the torrent of fierce, whooping Apaches which was now sweeping down upon them across the plain.

"Our lives are worth about as much as our title to that mine," said Steve; and it was no shame to him that he felt his young heart beat pretty rapidly.

"Sling your rifle behind you on the saddle; fold your arms; sit still. I'll do the talking."

The storm of dark horsemen was headed by Many Bears in person, and it was barely two minutes more before he was reining in his pony in front of the two "pale-face Lipans."

"How!" said Murray, quite heartily, holding out his right hand, with the open palm up, while he put his left upon his breast.

"How!" replied the chief, with a little hesitation; but a dozen voices around him were shouting,

"Send Warning!"

"Knotted Cord!"

"Pale-face friends of Apaches!"

And it was plain that the description given of them by Red Wolf and the girls had been accurate enough for their instant recognition.

"Other pale-faces run away. Why you stay?"

"Don't know them. Strangers. Run away from Apache chief. Chief must not follow."

"Why not follow?"

"Run against Lipans. Have big fight. Lose many warriors.

All for nothing. Better go back."

"Send Warning is a good friend. Do what he say. You come?"

"Yes—we come. Trust friend."

Steve listened in silent wonder. He had never heard Murray speak a word about the Apaches that was not full of distrust of their good faith as well as hate of their ferocity, yet here he was treating them with the most absolute confidence. Steve felt quite sure he would have hesitated, for his own part, to meet a band of Lipans in that way. He did not understand Indian character as well as Murray, in spite of his three years among them. A man who came to them conferring benefits, and betraying no doubt of their good faith, was as safe among them as if he had been one of their own people.

It also occurred to Steve that this was hardly what Murray had been sent out for by To-la-go-to-de, but his devotion to the interests of that chief was not strong enough to make him care much.

Whatever might be Murray's intentions, Steve was clear enough that his own would never carry him back to make any sort of report of their "scouting."

The Apaches wheeled toward the west, and Send Warning and Knotted Cord rode on at the side of Many Bears.

CHAPTER XVII

If To-la-go-to-de and his Lipans had moved forward just a little earlier that morning, they might have been in time to witness the departure of Captain Skinner and his men on their ill-advised expedition. As it was, they were astonished enough by what they saw.

"Pale-faces."

"Big wagons."

"Much horse. Much mule."

"No Tongue leave that behind him for Lipans to take, and go on after Apaches."

They believed they had solved one of their puzzles; but a good deal harder one was the question, "Who are those pale-faces, and where do they come from?" No such party had ever been known or heard of in that vicinity, and To-la-go-to-de instantly came to the decision that this one should never be heard of again.

"Not many," he said. "Ride straight down valley and eat 'em up. Plenty plunder. Carry back big present for squaw to look at."

William O. Stoddard

His eager warriors answered him with whoops and yells of approval, and he led them swiftly down all that was left of the pass and out into the valley.

It looked as if Murray had been altogether right when he sent word to Captain Skinner by Bill that there was "danger behind him." Bill himself was thinking of it at that very moment, and saying to one of his mates, "I'd about as lief see the sheriff and his posse, all the way from Denver."

"Well, yes, I'd a good deal ruther be arrested than scalped any day."

"Thar's a big swarm of 'em. No use for us to fight. I can't even lift my rifle."

"Try a little friendship. Maybe old Skinner'll tell ye you've been showin' good-sense agin."

"May save our scalps, boys; but I don't reckon it'll save us much of anything else."

"They're comin' right down onto us. If Skinner and all the boys were here, we could stop 'em, though."

If To-la-go-to-de's keen eyes had told him there were two dozen sharp-shooting white men in that camp, instead of three, he and his Lipans would never have dreamed of charging in as they now did.

It was not a very ceremonious or friendly way of making a morning call. There was a good deal too much noise about it. Too much clattering of lances and too many fierce, exulting war-whoops.

"Our time's come, Bill."

"It is if we anger them. Keep a steady eye, boys. Say 'How!'"

Those three miners were men of great courage, and their nerves must have been in the best of order, for they steadily walked out to the border of the camp and met the Lipans as if they had invited them to breakfast and were expecting them to come. There was just this difference, however, between their greeting of the Lipans and Murray's encounter with the Apaches: Bill and his two friends had sent no act of kindness and good-will ahead of them, while Murray and Steve were already firmly established, and well known as "friends of the Apaches, ready to fight for friends."

It was a very wide difference, but the three miners had acted wisely. The Lipan warriors in front of them lowered their lances, and the chief himself responded grimly to their "How!" But he did not offer to shake hands with them, and he did not check his braves in their rush through the camp and all over it.

"Don't tell 'em too much, Bill. The Captain and the boys won't be gone long. We can't warn 'em nuther."

That was just before old Two Knives gathered all the English he knew to question his prisoners. He saw at a glance that the men before him were only a part of a large party. The fires and the signs left of the breakfast which had been eaten were quite enough for that, not to speak of the size of the outfit.

"How many?" he asked.

Bill held up both hands, with the fingers spread, twice, and then one hand.

"Ugh! How hurt arm?"

"Fight with Apaches."

"Ugh! Good. Where gone? All pale-face braves?"

"Hunt Apaches. Out there."

"Ugh? Hope find 'em. Kill half. Lipans kill rest. Kill pale-face too. Put down gun. Prisoner this time. Shut mouth."

Bill had never in his life seen an uglier expression on the face of a man than was worn by that of the Lipan chief at that moment.

There was no use in resistance. Silently the three miners permitted themselves to be deprived of all their weapons; but the "stripping" stopped there. A brave who reached out his hand for the battered hat on the head of Bill was checked by To-la-go-to-de.

"Ugh! No want him. Let pale-face wear him. Take off scalp too, by-and-by."

There was nothing very cheering in that, but Bill's head did feel a little safer with the hat on.

"Tell ye what, boys," he afterward said to his mates, "when that redskin's hand teched the brim of that hat it felt as if the hull top o' my head was comin' loose."

It did not take those sixty Lipans long to find out all there was to be found in that camp. Their first and keenest interest was in the horses and mules, and the quality and number of these drew from them shouts of approval. The mules alone were worth any number of mustang ponies in a trade either with other Indians or with the border pale-faces.

Their first attempt at ransacking the wagons was sternly checked by old Two Knives.

"Maybe pale-faces got fire-water. To-la-go-to-de not want braves drunk now. Big fight maybe."

Every brave among them knew the good-sense of that, but they felt better satisfied a little later. The chief himself superintended a careful inspection of the wagons by two of his oldest sub-chiefs.

"He won't find a drap of any kind of liquor," growled Bill. "But I wish thar was some, and I could pisen it for him. They're a bad lot."

"Thar's too many on 'em for the boys to handle, I'm afraid."

"Captain Skinner's jest the man to try it and find out. Thar'll be a hot time, thar will!"

Two Knives probably had some such idea in his head, for his next orders, when carried out, left Bill and his two mates firmly bound to separate trees, so that no braves need be compelled to waste their precious time as "guards" over them.

The camp was now no longer the camp of the miners, it was that of the Lipans, and everything in it was their property, by all the laws of Indian warfare. There was yet to be at some future time, of course, a fair division of the plunder, but the "transfer" had been fully made and it was too late for anybody else to interfere.

It takes a great deal of civilization to make a South-western Indian, of any tribe, understand the white man's idea that his horse is still his own after it has been fairly stolen. To the

William O. Stoddard

Indian's mind, the theft gives the thief even a better title than he could acquire by paying money, and the biggest brave of any band is almost sure to be its most successful and renowned horse-thief.

The Lipans were specially well pleased over their morning's work, for they had won all that plunder without the loss of a single warrior.

The fate of the three prisoners was a matter to be thought over. To-la-go-to-de was by no means sure he had no farther use for them. He could wait till his braves should return from the examination he had ordered of the plain below the valley. It was less than an hour before they came back, and in a remarkable hurry, with the news of the approach of the main body of the pale-faces.

Old Two Knives merely nodded his head. His captives had told him the truth. But that number of white men would not be likely to attack at once so strong a band as his own. A full company of regular cavalry would hardly have been enough to scare him, for the Lipans are second to no other in their fighting qualities, and these were picked and chosen warriors.

"Pale-face come. Laugh at him."

Captain Skinner and his men saw nothing to laugh at when they rode near enough to understand the condition of affairs in their camp.

The blow had fallen upon them so suddenly that, for some moments after they halted on the plain, half a mile away, not a man could say a word.

"It's our fault, Cap. We ort to have follered your advice."

"Ort not to have left the camp."

"You was right."

"It's too late for that kind of talk, boys. The question for us is, what had we best do? Anybody got anything to say?"

There was another moment of glum, sulky silence, and then a perfect storm of angry outcries.

"Charge in on 'em!"

"Kill every soul of 'em."

"Fight right away."

"We won't lose all that's in them wagons."

"That'll do, boys. I know you've got all the grit for a fight," said Captain Skinner, "but suppose they're too much for us, and wipe us all out, what then?"

"Then that's what it'll have to be, Cap. We're ready."

"All right, boys. But no matter what comes, not a man of you must run. Not for a yard."

"We'll stand by ye, Cap."

"Most likely thar ain't no use talkin' of Bill and the boys."

"Not much, I reckon. They had no kind of show."

There was no time to do any mourning for their comrades, but the way in which that line of white horsemen now rode forward made the Lipans open their eyes in astonishment.

William O. Stoddard

"Keep about a rod apart," said the Captain. "Walk your horses. Don't fire a shot unless you've got a good aim at something. We'll draw them nigh enough to teach 'em a thing or two."

For once even old Two Knives, with all his cunning, was led into making a mistake. He was unwise enough to try and scare those miners, when there was not a man among them who knew how to be afraid, and they had all agreed to be killed rather than not whip those Lipans and get back what was in the wagons.

It was a bad mistake for those Indians to make even a threat of a charge, when it brought them in a pretty compact mass, just as they were about to wheel, instead of "charging," less than two hundred yards from the steady line of pale-faces.

"Now, boys, save every shot."

It was not a volley. The rifles cracked rapidly, one after another, but all were fired in a very few seconds and the Lipans recoiled in dismay, firing wildly as they went, and carrying off their dead and wounded.

"Keep it up, boys. Steady. Take a pony if you can't hit a redskin."

The "rally" of the Lipans was quickly made, and their own firing grew hotter, but it had little of the cool accuracy that Captain Skinner insisted on from his own men. All the while, too, he was moving steadily forward, and To-la-go-to-de began to understand what kind of men he had to deal with.

A sharp, deep-throated order to three of his braves was rapidly obeyed, and in a few minutes more the miners heard their Captain's voice, excitedly,

"Halt! They've brought out the boys. They've stopped firing."

It was precisely so. There were Bill and his two mates, on foot, with their arms tied behind them, and before each stood a Lipan, with his lance levelled, ready to strike.

"That's plain, boys. They've got their lesson. Don't want any more. Want a talk. They'll kill those three if we don't hold up."

"We've only lost two, Cap, and we've laid out more'n a dozen of them."

"Save the boys!"

"No fault of their'n."

"Have a talk, Cap."

"We'll have to give up something if we do. They'll never give us back the outfit."

"You know what we want. We're close to the border now."

"All right. I'll ride out. I reckon their chief'll come to meet me."

The meaning of the Lipans had been plain enough. The sudden firing of the miners upon their superior force had had all the effect of a surprise.

They were furiously angry over their losses, but their wise leader saw that he must give them a breathing-spell. No troops in the world could stand a fire so withering as that which came from the repeating-rifles of the desperadoes. Quite as many ponies as men had gone down, and their morning's plunder had already cost them more than it was worth. Therefore it must not be permitted to cost them any more, if they could help it by threats and talking.

CHAPTER XVIII

There was a good deal of beauty as well as convenience in the spot which the Apache braves had chosen for their camp on the bank of the river.

Many Bears had approved of it when he came in, but he had said nothing about the beauty of it. He had only ordered two or three trusty warriors to go at once and hunt for a ford, so that he could get upon the opposite bank of the river if necessary.

It was some little time before they found one, a mile lower down, and then they and the great chief were astonished by a report brought in to him by Dolores with his supper. Some of the squaws, she said, had taken their children into the river for a bath, right there by the camp, and one of them had found a place where she could wade across and back.

It was afterward found to be a flat ledge of rock, with deep water above and below, but it was none the less a bitter pill for the pride of the warriors.

To think of squaws and children presuming to find, right there under their noses, the very thing they were hunting for up and down so anxiously! That, too, when any man's eyes, or any woman's, could now perceive a good deal of a ripple

William O. Stoddard

in the water on the shallow place, such as ought to have made them suspect it at once.

Ni-ha-be's own eyes had been the first to notice that ripple, and she had set a couple of bright boys at the business of exploring it.

Of course the older squaws claimed the credit, when the ford was found, but Rita remarked to her sister,

"Let Too Many Toes say she saw it first. Too much talk. She'll be beaten again if she isn't careful."

"I saw it myself."

"I don't care. You and I have done enough, yesterday and to-day. We must keep still."

Rita was right, and Ni-ha-be knew it; but it was very hard to hear Too Many Toes so loudly assert her own acuteness and quickness of vision.

"She's the ugliest squaw in the whole band. Her children are ugly and her husband is too lazy to feed them, Rita."

"Hush. Father and the chiefs are coming. Walk away."

They did not go far and they were looking back all the while. Many Bears and his councillors marched dignifiedly down to the bank, and a tall brave walked right on into the river.

Not a word was spoken while he waded across and back, the water nowhere rising much above his waist, although it ran pretty swiftly.

His next business was to explore the width of the ledge, and that was found to be at least ten feet at the narrowest.

Long before that was done, however, Ni-ha-be had been reconciled to the policy of silence.

Too Many Toes could not be silent, and she disputed so loudly with another old squaw over their claim to the glory of finding that ford, that the chief and the councillors felt that something must be done for discipline.

Many Bears nodded sharply at the husband of Too Many Toes.

"Much noise. Warriors hear too big boasting. Teach squaw."

That was enough, and in a moment more the end of a heavy hide "lariat" or horse rope was falling rapidly upon the shoulders of the two offenders, Too Many Toes getting much the larger share of the beating. Her husband had been one of the braves who had wasted so much time in finding the other ford, and he agreed with his chief that somebody ought to be punished for it.

"Serve her right," said Ni-ha-be.

There was no question but what some kind of justice had been done, and that was a fair specimen of Apache household government.

If the poor, tired-out little mule who had served as an "omnibus" for Too Many Toes and her family happened to see the use made of that lariat, perhaps it comforted him too, for she had beaten him unmercifully all the way, and he was not her mule.

At all events, the discovery of the ford made that a safer

place for a camp. Orders were given not to put up any lodges or unpack any baggage until morning, and the whole band prepared for a night in the open air.

It was a complete "bivouac" but there was no hardship in it. The air was dry and warm. There was very little wind. The grass on which they could spread their blankets and buffalo-skins was deep and soft. Besides all that, and more important than anything else, they were all used to it, and would have laughed at anybody who imagined it a hardship.

Even Rita and Ni-ha-be never thought of such a thing, but after they lay down together it seemed more than usually difficult to get to sleep.

Nowhere in the world is the air more pure, and there were no clouds, nor was there yet any moon. The sky was all one blaze of stars, and the two girls could hardly help gazing at them.

"They're so bright," said Rita.

"I've seen them all before. Just as bright as they are now.

"So many of them, too."

"No more than there always is in good weather. When it rains hard it puts them out and they have to be lighted again."

"There is something about them in the talking leaves."

"What do they say?"

"I could not hear it all, but I understood some of it. The wise pale-faces look at the stars and know all their names. All the tribes of them and families."

"Tribes and families! I don't believe it. They're all one tribe, and they all shine for the Apaches." There was no denying that, and Rita had not read or understood enough to say much more.

Long after Ni-ha-be was sound asleep, however, her adopted sister was lying wide-awake, and staring at all that glory overhead.

"I remember now. It was my father told me about the stars. That's why I knew what the talking leaves meant. He was very good to me. I can see him plainer and plainer all the while."

It was a matter of course that one memory should bring back another, but they were all pretty cloudy as yet. Not bright and clear like the great stars, but misty and dim like those white streaks in the sky.

Rita gazed and gazed and thought and thought, until at last her eyelids closed heavily, and she too was asleep. Not so soundly as Ni-ha-be, for many strange dreams came to her, and all she could remember of them was the very last and latest of all.

It was just like the picture which Many Bears had spoken about the day before, only that now the miners did not look like that, and Rita in her dream actually thought she saw Many Bears himself among the Indians who were attacking them.

"He said he was there. I see him. They are coming! The squaw I saw in the book! Mother!"

And suddenly Rita found herself wide awake, and all the rest of her dream was lost to her.

William O. Stoddard

Ni-ha-be too was awake.

"What is the matter, Rita?"

"Oh, a dream!"

"Ugh! I never dream. That's the talking leaves. Dreams are big lies like them. What was it?"

"The fight in the picture."

"Miners? Pale-faces? Look, Rita, the braves are mounting to ride away. It is hardly sunrise, but they are going. Did your dream say there was any danger coming to us?"

"No, it did not say."

"I don't care. The Apaches are warriors, and Many Bears is a great chief. He will not let an enemy come near his camp."

"Besides, we can cross the river."

"Yes, by my ford."

"Ni-ha-be, remember what came to Too Many Toes!"

"She talked too much—when the chief and the braves were troubled in their minds. I know better than to do that. I'll talk to you, though. It's my ford!"

Mother Dolores was already busy at the nearest camp-fire, for she had not allowed the great chief to ride away without a nice bit of something to eat. Meaner braves could go hungry or pick a cold bone as they rode along. Not so the mighty husband of Dolores, the best cook of the Apaches. She knew too well where all her importance and dignity came from, and Many Bears was particularly glad to get his hot venison-steak that morning. No orders were left behind with reference to moving the camp, but all the second-rate braves and half-grown boys were busying themselves over their weapons and ponies with as much importance in their manner as if they had been so many chiefs.

Some of them were well armed with repeating-carbines and good revolvers. Others had old and inferior guns. Many of the "boys" had nothing but bows and arrows, but they knew how to use them, and there is nothing much more effective in a close fight. Nothing except a revolver or a lance, and they all had lances.

On the whole, it was clear that Many Bears could muster quite a strong "reserve," as the soldiers call it, after all his tried and chosen warriors had ridden away with him at their head.

The fighting fever seemed to be spreading after breakfast, and the squaws too got out their bows and arrows, and so did the smaller boys. It looked as if any enemy who should ride into the camp of that band of Apaches that day would find it a sort of hornets' nest, with all the hornets, big and little, practising their stings.

Ni-ha-be and Rita were like the rest, and more than one "young brave," who had never yet been in any kind of a battle, looked enviously at the pretty young chief's daughter who could already boast of having sent an arrow through the arm of a full-grown paleface warrior, and helped defeat him and his dangerous companions.

That was a bright feather for the cap of any Indian girl, and she had been compelled to tell the story of it over and over again to the other squaws.

They came to hear it over now, for it was closely connected in their minds with the warlike preparations and the evident anxiety of their chief.

"Ugh!" scornfully remarked old Too Many Toes. "Pale-face have soft arm. Hold it up for little girl to shoot at. Then laugh at her. S'pose pale-face come here. I show 'em."

"Yes," rejoined Ni-ha-be, with a flash in her black eyes. "Pale-face look at you, see your face, run right away. Afraid you'll talk. Hear you once, then they never come again."

The laughter among the other squaws sounded as if they were not disposed to admire Too Many Toes, but she had something else to say.

"Little girl take prisoners and then let them go. Just like pale-face blue-coat. No sense. I kill every one. You see!"

"You?" said Ni-ha-be. "The only prisoner you ever took was a little rabbit of a mule. He's alive now. You couldn't even talk him to death."

"She talks too much now," added a dignified middle-aged squaw. "Get beaten again. We want to know what's coming. Warriors keep it all to themselves. Did Ni-ha-be hear of many pale-faces?"

"No. Heard Send Warning tell Red Wolf there is danger coming. Believe what he said. Great chief and all the old men believe too. Good friend. Young warrior good friend too. Come see us some day. Squaws cook big dinner."

The questioning was by no means over, but the mention of her last beating silenced Too Many Toes. Public opinion was against her, and there were a good many others who had something to say.

Rita, too, came in for her share, and it was remarkable how closely she and Ni-ha-be were able to describe every article of clothing worn by their two white friends and their three white enemies, with the color of their eyes and hair, and every noticeable thing about their arms and equipments. The girls had eyes of their own, and they had used them to good purpose. The fact is, Indians can read almost everything excepting books.

William O. Stoddard

CHAPTER XIX

Many Bears did not seem disposed to hurry his return to his camp after his meeting with Steve and Murray.

Perhaps he was the more willing to ride slowly because it gave him an opportunity to ask a great many questions, and to consider the answers given. He did not seem very curious as to the past history of his new friends. Indian politeness compelled him to let them keep their own affairs to themselves. Besides, the account they gave sounded well.

"Send Warning and Knotted Cord find mine? Ugh! Good. Apache not want him. Friend keep him. Then other pale-face come for mine? Ugh! Bad. Drive off friend. Too many rifle. Too many big strong. You not like it. Ugh! Apaches drive 'em all away. Take every scalp. You see."

"We're in no hurry about the mine," said Murray. "Stay away now. Go back for it some day. Too many Lipans."

"They go away too. Go beyond mountains. Never come over here before. Apaches must teach 'em a lesson."

That was the great trouble in the mind of Many Bears at that moment. He wanted to travel westward as fast as possible, and yet here was a band of his tribe's worst and most ancient enemies within easy striking distance. Not to speak of Captain Skinner and his men, and the "plunder" there might be in their "outfit." He felt that it was no small thing to be a great chief, and to be compelled to decide questions of such importance.

"What you say? Send Warning tell friend what do."

"Let 'em all alone," said Murray, promptly. "Maybe Lipans fight pale-faces. Maybe not. Both get scared and go away. No good to lose warrior for nothing."

"Get scalp. Get big name. All tribe say great chief!" That was the difficulty. His pride was in the way of his good-sense.

Murray did his best in the remainder of that ride, and he might perhaps have succeeded in his peaceful advice, if it had not been for the hot temper of the younger braves and the "war spirit" they found at the camp on their arrival.

"They're a venomous lot," said Murray to Steve, as he looked around him while they were riding in. All the mixed "reserve" who could get ponies had mounted them and ridden out to meet their chief and his warriors. More than one squaw was among them ready to ply bow and arrows, or even a lance, if need should be.

"Well," replied Steve, "I reckon an arrow hurts just as much when a squaw sends it."

"They shoot best on foot."

"I don't see why. I never saw a Lipan squaw in a fight."

"I have, then. I've seen 'em sit down, put their feet on the bow, and send an arrow farther than any brave could send it drawing with his hands. Look at some of those bows. Could you bend them?"

"I never tried it sitting down. I've seen a Lipan squaw use a lance, but it was on a buffalo."

"Do you suppose that ugly old vixen yonder doesn't know how to handle the one she's carrying? They're terribly unmerciful in a fight."

"I'd hate to fall into her hands, before a fight or after one."

"After one would be the worst. Such squaws as she is are the most cruel tormentors of prisoners."

The face of Too Many Toes was again against her, for the lance-bearer was no other.

Alas for her, however!

The warrior to whom the lance belonged, and who also owned the pony she was riding, caught sight of her at that moment, and instantly galloped out from his place in the returning column. He did not listen for a moment to the shrill outcry with which he was greeted, or to her assertion of her readiness to fight the enemies of the Apaches.

The lance was wrested from her, and she was roughly unseated from the pony.

"Go get mule," said the contemptuous brave. "Put heap pappoose on him. Squaw warrior not wanted just now."

"There!" said Ni-ha-be to Rita. "Too Many Toes is in trouble again. I was watching her."

"Where are your eyes, Ni-ha-be? Don't you see who is coming?"

"Father? All the braves? Oh, Rita, there are Knotted Cord and Send Warning! They have come to visit their friends."

"I was looking at that ugly old squaw. I hope she will get beaten again."

Not this time, for she had hastened away at once on being deprived of her borrowed pony. Her offence against the laws of property of an Indian village was covered by the apparent circumstances, or it might have been worse for her.

It was no time for any squaw, old or young, to make herself noticeable, and the two girls kept themselves almost out of sight in the crowd.

They did not so much as guess how eagerly their faces were all the while sought for by the eyes of those two pale-faces.

"Do you see them, Murray?" had been the first thing Steve had said, as they were riding in.

"Not yet. Be careful, Steve. If you see them you must not speak to them. Contrary to rule."

"Not speak to them?"

"Not till the chief himself introduces you. Even after that you must not say too much."

"Well, yes. I suppose they are jealous about their squaws. Just like the Lipans."

"That's it, exactly. All Indians are. Besides, you are a young brave and a pale-face. They may not be quite so particular about a white-headed old warrior like myself."

"I'm white. I'll speak if I get a chance."

"And get kicked out of the village for it, or worse? No, my boy, you must be prudent. You haven't been asked to make yourself at home as yet."

Steve did not want to make himself at home, but he was well pleased, as he looked around him, to see how very strong was that band of Apaches. It seemed as if he had just so much more reason to feel safe about again falling into the hands of the Lipans.

True, he was among the wildest kind of wild Indians, but he was not a prisoner here, and the Apaches had no claim on him.

"They will not care whether I go or stay," he said to himself.

He had not gotten away from them yet, however, and among the first to welcome him was the haughty presence of Red Wolf.

Steve did not know that Ni-ha-be had already stirred up her brother on his account.

"Knotted Cord saved your scalp," she said to him "Now he comes to visit you, and you are too proud to speak to him. You are no better than a pale-face."

"Red Wolf is young. He must wait for his turn. The old men would push him back."

"No, they won't. They will keep Send Warning to talk to

them. Knotted Cord is young. His head is brown, not white."

There was something in that, and Red Wolf did not wait till the formal reception of the two white visitors was attended to. He said to his father,

"Knotted Cord is mine. He must eat my venison."

"Ugh! Young braves. Been in same fight. Good. Dolores cook deer-meat for him. Old warrior stay with chiefs. Ugh!"

It was precisely as Ni-ha-be had expected, and Red Wolf was the proudest young brave in camp when he held out his hand to Steve and found it grasped so very heartily.

Steve was glad to see him, and showed it, and so did Murray. The latter, indeed, won the heart of Many Bears by saying of his son, in the presence of the warriors standing by, "Brave young man. Stand right up and fight. Make a great war-chief some day. I like him."

Such testimony from a man who had given proof of his own prowess, and who was, as their keen eyes told them, himself a great warrior, did wonders for the fame of Red Wolf. It was almost as much as if he had taken and brought home a scalp.

"Young men go," said Many Bears. "Send Warning stay with gray heads."

Steve walked away at his new friend's side, both of them a little puzzled what to do or say, until Steve asked a question in Mexican Spanish.

The ice was broken. Red Wolf understood that tongue as well as Steve did.

"You are my brother. You are not a pale-face."

Steve was not altogether ignorant of Indian manners, and of their bitter prejudices, and he replied,

"Brother? Yes. All right. I am an Apache now. Fight for tribe. Fight for brother."

That was precisely what he had already done, so that it was more than a mere profession; but the reply of Red Wolf had a great deal of frankness in it.

"Red Wolf is an Apache. His father is a great chief. He hates pale-faces. Glad his brother has come to be an Apache. Eat with him now. Show him foolish young squaw that ran away and got caught. Squaw know very little."

They had walked along for some distance, and when Red Wolf said that he was very near his own campfire. He had not intended it for any ears but those of Steve Harrison, and his pride forbade his noticing the ripple of laughter which immediately followed it. Not even when he heard Ni-ha-be say, in her own dialect,

"Did you hear him, Rita? He was one of the braves who went to find the ford. They forgot to ask the squaws where to look for it."

Steve heard the rippling laugh, but he did not understand the words. Could they be making fun of him? His cheeks burnt red-hot at the thought of it, for he turned his head just long enough to see that those two pairs of bright and searching eyes were looking straight at him. They dropped instantly, but not before they had seen the quick flush rise to his face.

"Ni-ha-be," whispered Rita, "he will think we are rude."

"Ni-ha-be—Rita," said Red Wolf at that moment, "tell Dolores she must cook for the Knotted Cord. The chief says so. Bring blanket. Bring water. Be quick."

Dolores was near enough to hear, and she was perfectly willing. It was a post of honor to cook for a guest of Many Bears. The girls, too, were ready to bring gourds of drinking water, blankets to sit down upon, or do anything else which could properly be asked of two young Apache ladies of their high rank.

"Rita," said Ni-ha-be, while they were dipping their water-gourds in the river, "he is as handsome as an Apache."

"He is not nearly so good-looking as Send Warning. He is a mere boy."

"Can he see to talk with the talking leaves? His eyes are very good."

"I don't know; I will find out. Send Warning is a wise man— I am sure he is. They will talk to him. He is old, and the snow is on his head."

"Father says the snow is bad on a head sometimes. Every thing dies under it. Head good for nothing."

The two girls were getting up a good deal of partiality concerning their white friends and visitors, but they both stood gravely and silently enough before Red Wolf and the Knotted Cord when they brought them the water.

"Young squaws thank you for help," said Red Wolf. "Both very glad. Very young. Very foolish. Daughters of great chief himself."

Steve almost forgot Murray's caution, for he frankly held out his hand, saying,

"I'm glad Murray and I were on hand to help them. They're too nice to be killed. Glad to see them both well."

Mother Dolores was looking on, and was deeply scandalized by the terrible boldness of Ni-ha-be, for that young lady actually took the hand Steve held out and shook it, for all the world as if she had been a brave. Such a thing was unheard of, and what made it worse was the fact that Rita instantly followed her sister's example.

Red Wolf hardly knew what to say, but he was pretty well used to seeing Ni-ha-be have her own way. He was pleased that they had stopped short of so grave an offence as speaking.

"Rita will go. She will bring the talking leaves by-and-by. Red Wolf has a question to ask of his brother. Ni-ha-be go too."

Steve would have been glad of a longer call upon the daughters of the great chief, but they quietly walked away, as became them, not even laughing until they were at some distance.

Then it was Ni-ha-be who laughed, for Rita was thinking about the talking leaves, and wishing with all her heart that she could manage to ask some questions of her own concerning them.

"If he could not answer me, I am sure Send Warning could. He is old, and he is wise, and I know he is good."

CHAPTER XX

The trees to which Bill and his two mates had been tied by the Lipans were so situated that all that they needed was to turn their heads in order to have a good view of what was doing on the plain to the westward. They saw their captors ride out, and heard their whoops and yells of self-confidence and defiance.

"Don't I wish I was with the boys just now!" growled Bill.

"Three more good rifles'd be a good thing for 'em."

"Skinner'll fight, you see'f he don't. He'll stop some of that yelling."

"He's great on friendship and compromise," groaned Bill. "He may think it's good-sense not to shoot first."

The three gazed anxiously out toward the scene of the approaching conflict, if there was to be one. They could not see the advance of their comrades, but they knew they were coming.

"Hark!" suddenly exclaimed Bill. "That's the boys. Opened on 'em. Oh, don't I wish I was thar!"

The other two could hardly speak, in their excitement and disgust. It was a dreadful thing for men of their stamp to be tied to trees while a fight was going on which might decide whether they were to live or die.

Suddenly a squad of Lipans came dashing in. The cords that bound them were cut—all but those on their hands—and they were rudely lifted upon bare-backed ponies and led rapidly away to the front of the battle.

They could not understand a word of the fierce and wrathful talking around them, but the gesticulations of the warriors were plainer than their speech. Besides, some of them were attending to wounds upon their own bodies or those of others. Some were on foot, their ponies having been shot under them. More than all, there were warriors lying still upon the grass who would never again need horses.

"It's been a sharp fight," muttered Bill, "for a short one. I wonder if any of the boys went under? What are they gwine to do with us?"

A tall Lipan sat on his horse in front of him, with his long lance levelled, as if only waiting the word of command to use it. It remained to be seen whether or not the order would be given, for now To-la-go-to-de himself was riding slowly out to meet Captain Skinner.

"He can't outwit the Captain," said one of the miners. "Shooting first was the right thing to do this time. Skinner doesn't make many mistakes."

It was their confidence in his brains, rather than in his bones and muscles, which made his followers obey him, and they were justified in this instance, as they had been in a great many others.

The greetings between the two leaders were brief and stern, and the first question of old Two Knives was,

"Pale-faces begin fight. What for shoot Lipans?"

"Big lie. Lipans take our camp. Tie up our men. Steal our horses. Ride out in war-paint. Pale-faces kill them all."

The chief understood what sort of men he had to deal with, but his pride rebelled.

"All right. We kill prisoners right away. Keep camp. Keep horse. Kill all pale-faces."

"We won't leave enough of you for the Apaches to bury. There's a big band of them coming. Eat you all up."

"The Lipans are warriors. The Apaches are small dogs. We are not afraid of them."

"You'd better be! If you had us to help you, now, you might whip them. There won't be so many of you by the time they get here. Pale-faces are good friends. Bad enemies. Shoot straight. Kill a heap."

Captain Skinner saw that his "talk" was making a deep impression, but the only comment of the chief was a deep, guttural "Ugh!" and the Captain added,

"Suppose you make peace? Say have fight enough. Not kill any more. Turn and whip Apaches. We help."

"What about camp, wagon, horse, mule, blanket? All kind of plunder."

"Make a divide. We'll help ourselves when we take the

Apache ponies. You keep one wagon. We keep one. Same way with horses and mules—divide 'em even. You give up prisoners right away. Give 'em their rifles, and pistols, and knives. Give back all you took from them."

"Ugh! Good! Fight Apaches. Then pale-faces take care of themselves. Give them one day after fight."

That was the sort of treaty that was made, and it saved the lives of Bill and his mates for that day at least.

It was all Captain Skinner could have expected, but the faces of the miners were sober enough over it.

"Got to help fight Apaches, boys."

"And lose one wagon, and only have a day's start afterward."

"One wagon's nothing, boys. All we care much for is in the wagon we'll choose to keep. As to the rest of it, we'll see about that. Did any of you get hurt besides Smith and Gorham?"

"Not a man. But there's two less to divide with if we ever git safe into Mexico."

The chief had at once ridden back to announce the result to his braves, and they, too, received it with a sullen approval which was full of bitter thoughts of what they would do to those pale-faces after the Apaches should be beaten, and the "one day's truce" ended.

The three captives were at once set at liberty, their arms restored to them, and they were permitted to return to the camp and pick out, saddle, and mount their own horses.

"The Captain's got us out of our scrape," said Bill. "I can't guess how he did it."

"Must ha' been by shootin' first."

"And all the boys do shoot so awful straight!"

That had a great deal to do with it, but the immediate neighborhood of the Apaches had a great deal more. To-la-go-to-de knew that Captain Skinner was exactly right, and that the Lipans would be in no condition for a battle with the band of Many Bears after one with so desperate a lot of riflemen as those miners.

The next thing was to make the proposed "division" of the property in and about the camp. The Lipan warriors withdrew from it, all but the chief and six braves. Then Captain Skinner and six of his men rode in.

"This my wagon," said Two Knives, laying his hand upon the larger and seemingly the better stored of the two.

"All right. We'll take the other. This is our team of mules."

So they went on from one article to another, and it would have taken a keen judge of that kind of property to have told, when the division was complete, which side had the best of it. The Lipans felt that they were giving up a great deal, but only the miners knew how much was being restored to them.

"It was worth a fight, boys," said Captain Skinner, when the saved wagon was hauled out among them. "There's a little spring of water out yonder beyond the bushes. Not as good as the other, but it'll serve our turn."

There was little or no mourning over their two fallen

companions. Each man felt that his own life was worth a good deal less than he had thought that morning, and there was no telling when his turn might come.

As for the Lipans, they were disposed to be sulky over the day's operations, for they could not disguise the fact that they had been pretty roughly handled by an inferior force. It was as sure as anything could be that they would take the first opportunity which might come to "square accounts" with the miners. Indeed, Captain Skinner was not far from right when he said to his men,

"Boys, it'll be a bad thing for us if the Apaches don't show themselves to-morrow. We can't put any trust in the Lipans."

"Better tell the chief about that old man and the boy," said one of the men.

"I hadn't forgotten it. Yes, I think I'd better."

It was easy to bring old Two Knives to another conference, and he received his message with an "Ugh!" which meant a good deal. He had questions to ask, of course, and the Captain gave him as large an idea as he thought safe to give of the strength and number of the Apaches.

"Let 'em come, though. If we stand by each other we can beat them off."

"Not wait for Apaches to come," said To-la-go-to-de. "All ride after them to-night. Pale-faces ride with Lipans."

That was a part of the agreement between them, but it had not been any part of the intention of Captain Skinner.

"We're in for it, boys," he said, when he returned to his own camp and reported. "We must throw the redskins off to-night. It's time for us to unload that wagon. We're close to the Mexican line. Every man must carry his own share."

"Guess we can do that."

"I don't believe we can. It'll be as much as a man's life's worth to be loaded down too much, with all the riding we've got before us."

"We won't leave an ounce, if we can help it."

"Well, not any more'n we can help."

It was strange sight, a little later, the group those ragged, weather-beaten men made around their rescued wagon, while their leader sat in front of it, with a pair of scales before him.

"Some of the dust is better than other some."

"So are the bars and nuggets."

"Can't help that," replied Captain Skinner. "Everything's got to go by weight. No assay-office down in this corner of Arizona."

So it was gold they were dividing in those little bags of buckskin that the men were stowing away so carefully. Yellow gold, and very heavy. Pockets, money-belts, saddle-bags, all sorts of carrying places on men and horses, were brought into use, until at last a miner exclaimed,

"It's of no use, boys. I don't care to have any more load about me—'specially if there's to be any running."

"Or any swimming," said another.

William O. Stoddard

"Swimming! I've got enough about me to sink a cork man."

"And I've got all I keer to spend. Enough's as good as a feast, I say."

One after another came to the same opinion, although Captain Skinner remarked,

"We're not taking it all, boys. What'll we do with the rest?"

"Cache it. Hide it."

"For the Lipans to find the next day? No, boys; we'll leave it in the wagon, under the false bottom. That's the safest place for it, if any of us ever come back. No redskins ever took the trouble to haul a wagon across the mountains. It'll stay right here."

The "false bottom" was a simple affair, but well made, and there was room between it and the real bottom of that wagon to stow a great deal more than the miners were now leaving.

They would have had no time to dig a hiding-place in the earth if they had wanted to, for messengers came from To-la-go-to-de before sunset to tell them he was nearly ready to start, and from that time forward the keen eyes of strolling Lipan horsemen were watching every step that was taken in the camp of their pale-face allies.

"If they want to know how much supper we eat," said the Captain, "we can't help it. I only hope I can blind 'em in some way before morning."

The supper that was eaten was a hearty one, but there was no use in providing any great weight of provisions to carry with them. Every man and horse had already enough to carry, and the largest and heaviest men were most in doubt as to whether they had better take any provisions at all.

CHAPTER XXI

As Steve walked away with Red Wolf, Many Bears at once turned his attention to Murray and the great affairs to be decided by the chiefs and councillors.

For himself, the first idea that called for expression was suggested by a faint odor of something broiling on the coals just in front of Mother Dolores.

"Send Warning ride long way. Get very hungry. Come. All great braves eat a heap."

If the power to eat very nearly as fast, for a given time, as Dolores herself could cook, was a sure mark of greatness, Many Bears had no superior in his own band. It had not made a fat man of him yet, but there was no telling what it might do for him in the course of time.

The chiefs and warriors whose fame and rank entitled them to such a privilege soon gathered for the expected "talk," and there were some of them whose busy squaws ventured to bring them supplies of provisions, but the greater number were contented to wait a while.

Murray found himself regarded as an honored guest. Not only were his hosts indebted to him for past favors, but they were anxiously expecting more. Indians are just like other human beings in such matters. Always ready to give a good dinner to a man from whom they expect something. To be sure, all they were now looking for was good advice, and sometimes people are not willing to give much for that. There was plenty to eat, and with it a great deal of dignity. Even questions were asked slowly and carefully, and every answer was thoughtfully considered before any comment was made upon it. At first Murray merely listened as brave after brave replied to the mention of his name. He saw that only the very gray-headed men had anything to say in favor of peaceful action and a prompt "getting away." He was even surprised at the warlike ardor with which many of the warriors declared their eagerness for a blow at the Lipans, and the good reasons they were able to give.

The presence of the band of Two Knives was a sort of invasion of the Apache hunting-grounds. The Lipans had no business this side of the mountains. They had come to strike the Apaches, and if they should be allowed to get away unhurt they would surely come again. Send Warning had already told how many there were of them. If there were no more than that, none of them ought to be allowed to get away.

Murray could but think that a party of Apaches in the Lipan country would probably be talked about and dealt with very much in the same way; but it seemed to require a special effort for him to think at all. His head had been in a sort of whirl for some minutes before the time when Many Bears turned suddenly upon him with the question,

"What Send Warning say? His head is very white."

Murray was muttering to himself at the moment, while Dolores handed her husband a stick with a piece of corn bread on the point of it, "She is not an Apache; she is a full-blooded Mexican. Yes, I've seen that woman before—" But the chief's inquiry startled him out of that train of recollection. He could not have answered instantly to save his life, but it was according to Indian notions that he should not speak too quickly, so he had time to recover himself.

"More enemies besides Lipans," he said at length. "Apaches better not forget pale-face miners."

"Ugh!"

The exclamation went all around the circle, for that was the very thing none of them had mentioned.

"Pale-faces fight Lipans," remarked Many Bears.

"Is the great chief sure of that?" asked Murray. "Suppose they come all together. Apaches need more braves then. Suppose they fight each other first, then Apaches eat up all that are left. Great chief better find out."

"Ugh!"

It was a very loud grunt indeed to come from the throat of Many Bears, and the chiefs and braves looked at one another in a way that spoke a good deal for the value they set on the advice of their white friend.

Whipping sixty Lipans was one thing; attacking them with a strong force of pale-face riflemen to help them was quite another.

"What Send Warning say do?"

"Do?" almost sharply exclaimed Murray, with his eyes upon

the retreating form of Mother Dolores. "I'll tell you. Send your whole camp across the river. They can surround it here. Then send out your best braves to watch for the Lipans. They'll attack you before morning. That's what they came for. They won't fight the miners."

He was partly right and partly wrong, but Many Bears and his chiefs rose to their feet as one man.

"The words of Send Warning are wise. He is very old, and he is a chief. No use talk any more. All braves go and eat a heap. Tell squaws bring up all ponies. Get ready to cross river. No lose time."

Murray was not a "general," and he had never studied war, but he knew it would be a good thing to have deep water between that camp and any assailants instead of behind it. Many Bears was a chief of great experience, but it had never occurred to him that it would cost him all his horses if he should be beaten in a fight with a river behind him. The blunder was remedied now with a rapidity which astonished even Murray, for he had not known how good a ford there was right there.

"Hope the Lipans won't find that out," he said to himself. "They'll think twice before they try to swim their horses. I've given these fellows good advice. May prevent a battle. But if one should come, how could I fight the Lipans? What am I doing in an Apache camp anyhow? Steve and I must make haste out of this."

And then a puzzled, pained, anxious look came over his wrinkled face, and he seemed to be looking around him very wistfully indeed, as if he wanted to see somebody.

"Not to-night, perhaps; but I'll see her again in the morning.

Steve and I must get away to-morrow. It'll be easy enough to give him his directions, and I can find Two Knives and his braves in a few hours."

Murray was a good deal upset by something or other, and it may be he had not quite made up his own mind what his difficulty might be.

As the deepening gloom of the evening settled slowly down he stood beside Many Bears on the bank of the river, and watched the young braves drive in the last squads of ponies from their pasturage and urge them across the ford. He had no idea how much quiet fun Steve and his friend Red Wolf had already enjoyed in a very similar occupation. The squaws had insisted upon making all the boys and girls who were big enough swim instead of going over on pony-back, and the youngsters in their turn had revenged themselves by doing all the mischievous pranks they knew.

Old Too Many Toes had been conspicuous in shoving small Indians into the water, and when at last she finished packing her little borrowed mule and a borrowed pony, there was a perfect swarm of "divers and duckers" around her. The water came well up the sides of the little mule, and she would not have minded that if the boys had been willing it should go no higher.

Even the solemn face of Many Bears himself expanded into a chuckle of dignified fun.

"Ugh! Squaw scold. Get spattered."

"Look!" said Red Wolf at the same instant. "Drop baby."

Not her pappoose, for it was safe under her blanket, but her three-year-old girl had slipped from behind her, and the river was sweeping it down stream.

"It will be drowned!" exclaimed Steve, in some excitement.

"No. Apache baby never sink. Swim a heap. Look!"

Steve looked, and there was no question but what the queer little thing was paddling bravely, and not even showing fear. To be sure, the current was carrying it away, but Steve now saw that three or four older boys and girls were swimming around it and were ready to give it all the help needed.

For all that, the wrath and anxiety of Too Many Toes exhibited itself in a torrent of long words.

Steve had learned among the Lipans that the red men have a great deal of fun in their compositions, but he was almost surprised to hear Red Wolf say, "Squaw talk big rain. Fall in river. Have freshet then. Lipans can't follow Apaches."

If talk could have raised the river, the chatter of nearly two hundred squaws of all ages, added to the scolding of Too Many Toes, would have made a torrent of it.

And yet a number of the squaws, wives and daughters of men of character and station attended to the business of fording the stream with the silence and gravity of the most dignified white matrons.

Dolores would have scorned putting herself on a level with such a squaw as Too Many Toes, even in the use of her tongue; and as for Ni-ha-be and Rita, they never forgot for a moment whose family they belonged to.

"Rita," said Ni-ha-be, as they rode down to the river, "your blanket is loose. Red Wolf and Knotted Cord are watching us."

"Send Warning is not there."

"No, of course not. He is with the chiefs. Don't let them see we are looking at them."

"I'm not looking at them."

"Neither am I. I don't care for Red Wolf either."

"And I don't care whether Knotted Cord sees me or not. I wish I could talk with Send Warning."

"What for?"

"To ask about the talking leaves."

"Knotted Cord could tell you. He is a pale-face."

"He is a mere boy. Send Warning's head is very white."

"Look out, Rita. Your horse's feet are slipping."

Ni-ha-be had better have been attending to the feet of her own pretty mustang. The ford was not very wide just there, and the two girls were compelled to get a little out of the way of the two mules loaded with lodge-poles.

Alas for the vanity of the chiefs self-confident daughter!

Her horse's fore-feet went over the ledge, and in an instant more she was floundering in the river, while every squaw and young Indian who could see her broke out into merry laughter.

It was well, perhaps, that she slipped from the ford on the up-stream side, but it was clear that she did not need a bit of help from anybody. No Apache girl of her age ever needed to be taught to swim. It was quite a credit to her, indeed, in the eyes of Steve Harrison, that she should so promptly catch her mustang by the head, turn it to the ledge, find her own footing on the rock, and encourage the unlucky quadruped to follow.

Then, although the water was at her shoulders, she managed, all dripping as she was, to clamber into the saddle again. It was so dreadfully provoking. She had heard Red Wolf laugh.

"Rita, did you look at them?"

"Look at whom? I was looking at you."

"Did they both laugh? Or was it only Red Wolf?"

"I don't know."

"Go on! Go on! Too Many Toes is saying something about me. She says it is her ford, and I fell in because I did not know where it was. Hurry on, Rita."

It was a sad blow to the pride of poor Ni-ha-be, but it need not have been. Any girl in the world might have had just such an accident befall her, but not a great many could have helped themselves out of it so skilfully and so bravely. That was precisely what Steve Harrison had been thinking, and he had not joined at all in the laughter of Red Wolf.

It had been the chief's order that the lodges should be set up on the safe side of the ford, and so there was work enough before the squaws. Even some of the younger braves were called upon to lend a hand, and in less than an hour's time there was a very respectable Indian village. Lodges, ponies, fires, dogs, everything belonging to an Apache hunting-camp was there, and between them and any probable danger the river was rolling now, and the Lipans did not know where to look for the ford.

"Ni-ha-be," exclaimed Dolores, sharply, a little later, "go into lodge. Too late for young squaw. What will the great chief say?"

"It is early yet."

"Go in. Lipans come and carry you off. Old pale-face see you, and say foolish young squaw. Not know enough to keep dry. Fall off pony. Ugh!"

That was a sharp hit, and Ni-ha-be obeyed Dolores rather than stay for another reminder of her ducking, but Rita followed her very slowly.

"If I could see him again," she murmured, "I feel sure he would speak to me. I don't care what they say. Dolores may scold as much as she pleases. I will ask Send Warning about those words, and all about those pictures."

She little guessed that at that very moment Murray was saying to Steve Harrison,

"Yes, Steve, she's pure white, but she's Indianized. Talks Indian. Thinks Indian. Don't know she's white."

CHAPTER XXII

To-la-go-do-de had all the pride of an Indian chief, but he had good reasons for respecting Captain Skinner. He had seen him handle his men in a fight, and he had talked with him afterward, and he knew that he had not beaten the Captain in either case. Now, therefore, that they were to go on a war-path together, he was not at all above a consultation with so wise and brave a leader.

For his own part, he had decided upon the right policy to follow. He had told his older warriors, "The pale-faces are cunning. The Lipans must be wise. Suppose the Apaches kill many pale-faces. Ugh! Good. Lipans kill rest of them very easy. Not so many to kill."

He was right about the Captain's "cunning," for it was a good deal like his own "wisdom," and it had been expressed to his men in the same way.

"The Apaches are strong enough to beat them and us too, and they'll be on the lookout. We mustn't throw ourselves away, boys. We must get separated somehow. There won't be enough Lipans left to follow us far."

He and Two Knives, therefore, had about the same object in view when they rode out together in advance of their

William O. Stoddard

combined force after supper. The sun was setting, but it would be a good while yet before dark.

The miners were all mounted, and nobody would have guessed how much extra weight they were carrying. They were drawn up now in a close rank in front of their little camp, in which they had not left a single guard. Two Knives asked about that.

"What for?" replied Skinner. "What good to leave men? If the Lipans want to rob wagon they kill the men we leave. Suppose Lipans do as they agree, camp safe? No. It will take all the men we've got to fight the Apaches."

That was good-sense, and Two Knives only said "Ugh!" to it; but his next question meant more.

"How about fight? Tell chief what do."

"No, I won't. It's your fight more than mine. If you want us to go ahead, we will go. If you say we are to keep back and let you go ahead, all right. If we say we want to do anything you will think it is crooked. Better not say. You say."

The chief had been expecting to hear some plan of action, and to find something "crooked" in it. Captain Skinner had beaten him at once and completely.

"Then you ride along with Lipans."

"No. The hearts of your young braves are hot and bitter. My men are angry. Must keep apart. Have fight among ourselves. No good."

There was no denying the good-sense of that, and Two Knives had no fear at all but what his pale-face allies would come back after their wagon, extra horses and mules. Of course they would stick to property for which they had shown themselves so ready to fight, and he could not suspect that they now had the best part of it carefully stowed away around them.

"Ugh! Pale-faces can't go ahead. Not stay behind. What then?"

"You say. We go."

"Ride left hand, then. Away off there. Not too far. We go this way. Both find Apaches. Come together then."

"All right. That'll suit us. Send some braves along to see that we don't run away."

Two Knives would have done so if Captain Skinner had not asked for it; but he instantly suspected a cunning plot for the destruction of as many braves as he might send, and he replied,

"Ugh! No good. Pale-faces take care of themselves to-night."

So both of them got what they wanted.

Two Knives believed that by keeping to the right he should make a circuit and surprise the Apache camp, while the miners would be sure to meet any outlying force by riding toward it in a straight line.

Captain Skinner's one idea was to get as far as possible from the Lipans, he hardly cared in what direction. To the "left" was also to the southward, and so he was better off than he had hoped for.

"Go slow, boys," he said to his men. "We must go right across every stream we come to. The more water we can put behind us the better."

The Lipans also advanced with caution at first, keenly watching the distrusted miners until they were hidden from them by the rolls of the prairie and the increasing darkness.

"Cap," said Bill, as they rode along, "why can't we turn now and win back the camp?"

"Yes, we could do it. And win another fight and lose some more men. Perhaps all of us. I'm not in any hurry for that."

The line on which the Captain was leading them slanted away more and more toward the south, but not so much as yet that it need have aroused the suspicions of To-la-go-to-de's keen-eyed spies who were keeping track of them.

They reached a good-sized brook, and the moment they were over it the Captain shouted,

"That gets bigger, or it runs into something before it's gone far. That's our chance, boys."

Nothing could be surer, for all the brooks in the world do that very thing.

Besides, that brook was running in the direction in which the miners wanted to go, and they now pushed forward more rapidly.

"If I knew where the Apache village was," said the Captain, "I'd go near enough to see if we could pick up some ponies. But we won't waste any time looking for it."

The men had plenty of comments to make, but not one of them was willing to set up his own judgment against that of the ragged little Captain. They would never have seen that village if it had not been for the river itself.

The brook was a true guide. In due time it led the miners to the place where it poured its little contribution into the larger stream, and that looked wider and gloomier by night than by day.

"No ford right here, boys. The water runs too still and quiet. We must follow it down."

"Why not follow it up, Captain?"

"Swamps. Can't you see?"

"Wall, no, I can't."

"I can, then. It's half a sort of lake. The river comes out of it. Lower down it'll run faster, and we'll find some shallow place."

"May run against Apaches."

"Got to take our chances."

There was no help for it, but every pair of eyes among them was as busy as the dim light would let it be, while they rode along the bank.

If they could but find a ford!

They thought they found one once, and a tall horseman wheeled his horse down the bank and into the placid water.

William O. Stoddard

"Careful, now. Feel your way a foot at a time," shouted Skinner.

"'Tain't three feet deep yet, and it's a good bottom."

It did not seem to get any deeper until he was half-way across, and the rest were getting ready to follow him, when his horse seemed to stumble and plunge forward.

There was a splash and a smothered cry, and that was all. Days afterward an Apache hunter found a stray horse, all saddled and bridled, feeding on the bank near the spot where he had swum ashore, but nobody ever saw any more of his rider. He had too many pounds of stolen gold about him, heavier than lead, and it had carried him to the bottom instantly.

"Boys," said Captain Skinner, "I'll try the next ford myself. I was half afraid of that."

Every man of them understood just what had happened, and knew that it was of no use for them to do anything but ride along down the bank.

There was not a great deal farther to go before a sharp string of exclamations ran along the line.

"See there!"

"Camp-fires yonder!"

"That's the Apache village!"

"It's on the other shore!"

"Hark, boys! Hear that—off to the northward? There's a fight going on. Ride now. We're away in behind it."

Captain Skinner was right again. By pushing on along the bank of the river he was soon in full view of the village, but there was very little of it to be seen at that time of night.

At the same time, just because he was so near it, he ran almost no risk at all of meeting any strong force of Apaches. The sound of far-away fighting had somehow ceased, but the Captain did not care to know any more about it.

"Silence, boys. Forward. Our chance has come."

He never dreamed of looking for a ford there by the village, and there were no squaws to find it for him or point it out. More than a mile below he came to the broad, rippling shallow the Apache warriors had reported to their chief, and into this he led his men without a moment's hesitation.

"Steady, boys; pick your tracks. Where the ripples show, the bottom isn't far down, but it may be a little rough."

A large part of it was rough enough, but Captain Skinner seemed to be able to steer clear of anything really dangerous, and in a few minutes more he was leading them out on the southerly shore.

"Now, boys," he said, "do you see what we've done?"

"We've got across the river," said Bill, "without any more of us gettin' drownded."

"That's so; but we've done a heap more than that. We've put the Apache village between us and the Lipans, and all we've got to do is to strike for the Mexican line."

That was all, and yet at least half of them had something to urge in favor of a night prowl around the Apache village, to see if they could not steal a few ponies.

"My load's gettin' powerful heavy, Cap," said one.

"We want pack ponies for our provisions," said another.

"After we get some."

"Boys," said Captain Skinner, "if that band of Apaches once gets on our track we won't need many more provisions. I'm going to give 'em as wide a berth as ever I can."

Again the Captain showed his superior wisdom, and he hardly permitted them to halt until the sun was rising. Just then the foremost man sent back a loud shout of,

"Here's another river!"

"That's all right," said Captain Skinner. "Now I know where we are."

"Where is it, then?" said Bill.

"The first river we forded was the north fork of the Yaqui, and this is the other fork. When we're on the other bank of that, we're in Mexico. We can go in any line we please then."

The whole band broke out into a chorus of cheers.

Whatever may have been their reason for wishing to get out of the United States, particularly that part of it, it must have been strong enough to make them anxious. They were not contented for a moment until this second "fork" was also forded.

"Cap," asked Bill, "is this Mexico, all around here?"

"I believe it is."

"Then don't you think we'd better go for a few Mexican deer? It's nigh breakfast time."

It would be necessary to hunt for something unless they were to starve. A good place for a camp was selected, the weary horses were unsaddled, all but the half dozen ridden by the hunters, and then the hungry miners could at last find time to "wonder if the Lipans are looking round that prairie after us."

"They won't find us," said Captain Skinner. "Start your fires, boys, I heard a rifle. One of them has struck his game quick."

So he had, but it was a queer kind of "Mexican deer." It had long, smooth, sharp horns and a long tail, and when the miners came to carve that venison one of them said,

"Boys, it's the first beef we've had in two months."

"Cap," said another, "do you reckon thar's a cattle ranch around here?"

"Not so near the Apache range as this is."

"How came this critter here, then?"

"I kin tell you," said the miner who had shot that tall, long-legged, long-horned Mexican steer. "Thar was more of 'em. Wild as buffler. This one wasn't even branded. They're just no man's cattle, they are."

"That's it," said Captain Skinner. "There are plenty of stray herds hereaway without any owner. The natives kill them whenever they want beef, just as we've killed this one. It isn't the best kind of eating, though. I'd rather look for a little deer-meat by-and-by."

Wild beef was better than nothing at all, however, and a busy lot of cooks were they for a long time after the first pieces of it were brought in.

They could talk, too, as well as eat, and the result of all their discussion was that they would do precisely as Captain Skinner had advised at the beginning of it.

"We sha'n't be safe, boys, till we get to some kind of town. We can scatter after that, but we'd best keep together for a while. This is a powerful uncivilized strip of country that we've got into. I've been down this way before, and I know what I'm talking about."

CHAPTER XXIII

If the Lipan chief could but have known, when he set out from his camp that evening, what had been determined on by Many Bears and his councillors, he might have proceeded more wisely. The Apache chief did not even go over the river, nor did any great number of his warriors. Those who went came back almost immediately, and Murray saw that nothing more could be done in behalf of peace.

"Send Warning come with braves?" inquired Many Bears, when at last his whole force was gathered, impatient to be led away.

"No. We two will stay and help take care of camp. Pale-faces make big peace with Lipans not long ago. Bad for us to strike them."

The chief could understand that.

An Indian of any tribe is held to be bound by the treaties made by his people. The younger braves sometimes forget their duty as completely as some young white men do, but an old warrior, a wise man, like Send Warning, was naturally expected to know better. He did not lose anything, therefore, in the good opinion of his new friends, and the only reply of Many Bears was, "Ugh! Good. Stay with camp. Lodge ready.

William O. Stoddard

Lipans never get near camp. All safe."

It might not have been so entirely safe, a few hours later, if Captain Skinner and his miners had known, when they passed it so nearly, that all its fighting population were then miles away on the prairie.

Not many miles, however, for Many Bears was thinking of Murray's assertion that his enemies would surely come to attack him, and he did not intend to let them get by him in the dark. They came pretty near it, after all, widely as the Apaches spread themselves, and keenly as they kept up their lookout.

To-la-go-to-de's grand "circuit" would have succeeded, and he would have dashed in upon the unprotected camp, if it had not been for a mere dwarf of a young brave who had stolen that opportunity to go on his "first war-path." He had done so without permission from his elders, and so kept well away from them, for fear some old warrior or chief might send him back to camp in disgrace.

Boy as he was, however, his ears were of the best, and he knew the sound of the feet of many horses. He heard them coming, and then he knew by the sudden silence that they had halted.

It was just at that moment that the spies of Two Knives came racing up to announce the suspicious change of direction on the part of the miners, and the chief was considering the matter.

"Not go back to camp?"

"No," said one of the Lipan braves, pointing toward the south. "All pale-faces go that way."

"Ugh. Good. Pale-face chief very cunning. Not want to run against Apaches. Go way around. Get there before we do. We ride."

The Apache boy had not waited for them to start again. He had promptly wheeled his pony and dashed away through the darkness with the news.

He had not far to go before he fell in with a squad of his own people, and his work was done. Older and wiser braves than himself, with eyes and ears as keen as his own, rode forward to keep watch of the advancing Lipans, while the others lashed their ponies fiercely away to spread the warning.

Many Bears had no notion of fighting so terrible an enemy with less than his whole force, and he was in no hurry to begin. Orders were sent for every body to fall back without being seen, and the Lipans were allowed to come right along, with the mistaken idea that they were about to make a surprise. It is bad to try such a thing as that and then be surprised yourself instead of astonishing anybody else.

The Lipans were moving in two long, scattered ranks, one about a hundred yards in advance of the other, expecting at any moment to come in sight of the camp-fires of the Apaches, or to meet some stray scout or other, when suddenly old To-la-go-to-de himself rose in his saddle, and sent back a low, warning cry. He had detected the neighborhood of enemies. He had seen shadowy forms flitting along in the gloom around him, and he was not sure but he had heard the beat of hoofs upon the sod.

In half a minute after he had uttered the warning cry which so suddenly halted his warriors, he was quite sure he heard such sounds, and a great many others.

First came a scattering but hot and rapid crash of rifle firing, then a fierce chorus of whoops and yells; and then, before the two ranks of Lipans could join in one body, a wild rush of shouting horsemen dashed in between them. There was a twanging of bows, a clatter of lances, more firing, with greater danger of somebody getting hit than there had been at first, and Two Knives found his little band assailed on all sides at once by superior numbers. The orders of Many Bears were that the rear rank of his foes should only be kept at bay at first, so that he could centre nearly all his force upon the foremost squad. The latter contained a bare two dozen of chosen warriors, and their courage and skill were of little use in such a wild hurly-burly. To-la-go-to-de and three more even suffered the disgrace of being taken prisoners, knocked from their ponies, tied up, and led away toward the Apache village. Had Captain Skinner and his miners been on hand, with all the Lipans they had killed or wounded, the result might have been different. But Captain Skinner was hurrying his men toward the ford, and nothing could restore to usefulness the warriors who had been smitten by their bullets.

The rear rank of the Lipans had made a brave charge at once, but it had taught them all they needed to know. That was a lost battle, and their only remaining hope was in the speed of their horses. They turned from that fruitless charge as one man, and rode swiftly away—swiftly, but not wildly, for they were veterans, and they kept well together. They were dangerous men to follow, and the main body of their foes was not yet ready to try it.

By the time old Two Knives and his three warriors were safely tied up, his fugitives' "rear rank" had galloped quite a distance, all the while successfully beating off the squads of "young braves" that annoyed them.

There is an old proverb that "a stern chase is always a long chase," and the Lipans were even better mounted than their pursuers. Besides, they all knew exactly what to do, and the night seemed to be getting darker, as if for their benefit. They could not mistake their way, and there were very few Apaches near them when they at last rode into their own camp.

There was no time for them to throw away in talking over their defeat, but they seemed to be united in their opinion that it was in some way due to bad faith on the part of Captain Skinner and his miners. If there was no time for anything else, therefore, enough could be spared for gathering the horses and mules of the pale-faces and setting their wagon on fire. They did the same with their own, after taking out of it all they could carry in any other way. They would have some good plunder to show on their return home, if they should get there, but what account could they give of the loss of their great war-chief and so many of his best braves, horses and all?

The Apaches were beginning to show themselves on the borders of the camp, and to send threatening whoops and distant shots into it, before the remnant of the Lipans were ready to move.

They sent their quadrupeds and wounded men ahead, toward the mouth of the pass by which they had entered that valley, and behind these the warriors rode sullenly along, every one of them longing for an opportunity to strike one more blow before he crossed the mountains. Nothing of the kind could be done that night, but there was no saying what might come into their angry minds before morning. They would have plenty of time to think after they were once safe in the pass, for their enemies would not dream of following them among the rocks.

CHAPTER XXIV

Even before the Apaches set out to find their Lipan enemies Murray and Steve made their way across the ford, and were guided by a bright-eyed boy to the lodge which had been set apart for them. That one had been given them at all was a mark of great respect; and this lodge belonged to Many Bear himself, which added to the honor done them.

"Now, Steve," said Murray, "you stay here awhile. I can do some things better if I'm alone."

"All right. But there's no danger of my going to sleep while you're gone."

"Pretty wide awake, eh? Well, it's an exciting time all around."

"It is for me, Murray. I feel as if I had made a good start on my way home."

"I guess you have. Your path is beginning to look pretty clear."

"I've escaped from the Lipans."

"But not yet from the Apaches. I can't say how soon I'll be

back again now, but you'd better not leave the lodge."

Steve threw himself down on the blanket he had spread upon the grass, and his thoughts came to him in a perfect crowd.

Sleep—for a boy like him, who had been for three years a prisoner, and was now getting free! He might as well have gone to sleep on his horse, if he had been out there among the warriors on the prairie.

Murray walked away from the lodge very slowly.

"It's not a bad place for a camp," he said to himself, "but that side of it is all bushes, and they have corralled all their loose ponies right in there. Old Many Bears will make some changes when he comes to see it. The squaws laid it out this time."

The lodges of the chief were not far apart from each other, and Murray had not gone twenty steps before he found himself in front of them and face to face with a very stout and dark-complexioned squaw. If she had been a warrior in the most hideous war-paint she could not have expected a man like Send Warning to be startled so at meeting her.

Perhaps she did not notice the tremor which went over him from head to foot, or that his voice was a little husky when he spoke to her. At all events she answered him promptly enough, for at that moment there was nobody in sight or hearing for whose approval or disapproval Mother Dolores cared a button.

She did not so much as give a thought to the youthful occupants of the lodge behind her.

If Ni-ha-be and Rita were not asleep they should be, and they were mere girls anyhow.

Ni-ha-be had not closed her black eyes for a moment, and Rita had only refrained from talking because of the presence of Dolores.

"I am glad she's gone, Rita. It's too bad we are shut up here, where we can't know a word of all that's going on."

"There will be noise enough when the chief and the warriors come."

"Or if the camp is attacked. My bow and arrows are ready."

"I don't believe we are in any danger. Hark! Ni-ha-be, don't speak."

"Somebody is talking with Dolores."

"Hark!"

They listened more and more eagerly, and they even crept to the outer edge of the lodge and gently raised the bottom of the deer-skin covering.

"Ni-ha-be, it is Send Warning."

Murray and Dolores were talking in Mexican Spanish. He was not saying anything about the Lipans, or anything else that seemed to Ni-ha-be very interesting. Neither did Rita understand why it should all be so much so to her, or why her heart should beat and her cheeks burn as she listened.

Murray had used his eyes to some purpose when he had watched Dolores at her cookery, and his first words had made her his very good friend.

"Squaw of great chief. Squaw great cook. Know how."

"Is Send Warning hungry?"

"Not now. Eat enough. Great chief and warriors go after Lipans. Pale-faces stay in camp."

"They will all eat a heap when they come back. Bring Lipan scalps, too."

"The Lipans are enemies of the Apaches. The Mexicans are friends."

"The Mexicans!" exclaimed Dolores.

"Yes. Great chief marry Mexican squaw. Handsome. Good cook."

"I am an Apache!"

"Yes, Apache now. Mexican long ago. Forget all about it. All about Santa Maria—"

"No, no; the talking leaf remembers that." And the poor woman nervously snatched from her bosom the leaf of the magazine on which was printed the picture of the Virgin and Child, and held it out to Murray.

He could but dimly see what it was, but he guessed right, for he said instantly,

"You remember that, do you? I suppose you never knew how to read. Not many of 'em do down there. The Apaches came one day and carried you off. Horses, mules, cattle, good cook—killed all the rest."

"How do you know?" suddenly interrupted Dolores. "I remember all that. Don't want to, but I can't help it. Same thing happen a great many times. Apaches are great warriors. Many Bears is a great chief. Bring back heap of prisoners every time."

She was telling Murray what he wanted to know, but he saw that he must ask his questions carefully, for, as he said to himself, "I never saw a woman so completely Indianized. She is more of an Apache than a Mexican now."

He talked and Dolores answered him, and all the while the two girls heard every word.

Ni-ha-be would have liked to make comments every now and then, and it was quite a trial to be compelled to keep so still, but Rita would not have spoken on any account. It seemed to her as if Dolores were telling all that to her instead of to Send Warning. She found herself thinking almost aloud about him.

"What a kind, sweet voice he has! He cannot speak Apache. I know he is good."

In another moment she again came near betraying herself, for the words were on her very lips before she could stop them and still them down to an excited whisper.

"He is not talking even Mexican now. It is the tongue of the talking leaves, and I can hear what he says."

More than that, for she soon found that she could repeat them over and over to herself, and knew what they meant.

Murray had talked to Dolores as long as was permitted by Indian ideas of propriety, and it was just as he was turning away from her that he said to himself, aloud and in English, "I am not mistaken. She is the same woman. Who would have thought she could forget so? I am on the right track now." And then he had walked pretty swiftly for a short distance, in a way that made Dolores wonder if he were not taken with some sharp and sudden pain. Then he stopped suddenly, and muttered,

"I don't care to see Steve just now. It is too bitter. I'll go down to the corral and see how our horses are getting along. We may need to have them in good condition to-morrow."

The horse corral was just beyond the line of bushes at the back of the lodges of Many Bears, and contained a good deal of wealth in the form of ponies and mules. Those of Murray and Steve were tethered to young trees, but with long lariats, so that they were feeding.

There was no one to watch Murray's movements. Only a brave of high rank would have presumed to go with him, and none of these were left in camp.

Steve Harrison, sitting alone in the lodge, staring out of the door at the smouldering camp-fires, and listening to the neighing of many horses and the barking of many dogs, wondered why his friend did not return, as the time went by, but could not guess at a reason. At last other sounds, distant but growing nearer, began to break in among those that belonged to the camp.

"Hear them whoop!" exclaimed Steve. "It isn't a fight, for there is no firing. Nothing but yells."

A great abundance of noise, to be sure, and it was rapidly coming toward the ford.

"The Lipans must have been beaten," said Steve, for he now saw that the Apache horsemen were crossing the river, and that every squaw and child in the village was pouring out to welcome them. "Squaws can do more whooping than the braves know how to. But I wonder what's become of Murray!"

It was but a few minutes before Red Wolf rode up to tell him the news, and ask him to come and take a look at the prisoners. It flashed across Steve's mind that it would not do for him.

"Lipans! They must not see me." And then he said aloud to Red Wolf, "I must wait for Send Warning. He may tell me I must not look upon them. He is my chief."

"Ugh! Good. Knotted Cord wait. Red Wolf go. Back soon."

As for Murray, he had not failed to hear the noise made by the triumphant braves on their return, and he had understood it better than Steve, for he exclaimed,

"That's the whoop for prisoners. If they bring in any, I must not let them see me here. I never hated Apaches more in my life. It won't do to lose my friends. Here they come."

He crept to the edge of the bushes and lay still. There would be a council called at once, he knew, and he would be sent for; but he was determined to wait and see what was done with the prisoners.

"That's one thing they will consult over. Hullo!"

He sunk down again in the bushes, for a squad of Apache warriors was approaching, bringing with them four men securely bound.

They were the great To-la-go-to-de and his three chiefs, neither of them hurt to speak of; but they were all that were left of the foremost rank of the Lipans in that brief, terrible combat.

Other braves kept back the swarming mob of squaws and children, while the four distinguished captives were almost carried into one of the lodges at the border of the bushes.

Here more thongs of strong deer-skin were tightened upon their helpless limbs, a strong guard of armed braves was stationed in front of the lodge, and the Lipans were left in the dark to such thoughts as might come to them.

Not an Apache among their guards dreamed that anything more dangerous than thoughts could or would come. And yet, within two minutes from the time he was spread upon his back and left alone, old Two Knives heard inside the lodge a low, warning hiss.

His companions also heard it, but neither of them was so unwise as to answer by a sound.

The hiss was repeated, and now it was close to the chief's ear.

"Friend come. No Tongue is here. Great chief must be snake. Creep through hole in back of lodge. Find plenty horse. Ride fast. Get to pass. Never forget friend. No Tongue come some time."

Even while he was whispering the sharp edge of Murray's knife was busy with the thongs, and in a moment more all four of the prisoners were free—free to lie silently while their friend repeated to each in turn his advice as to what they were to do next.

William O. Stoddard

Their nerves had not been shaken by their defeat, and when Murray slipped away again through the slit he had cut in the lodge cover, he was followed by four forms that made their way every bit as quietly as so many snakes could have done.

What puzzled To-la-go-to-de and his friends was that when they ventured to rise upon their feet, out in the dark among the horses, No Tongue was not with them.

"Ugh! Gone!"

"Cunning snake. Stay and strike Apaches. Then come."

"Good friend. Big warrior."

They could not quite understand the matter, but of one thing they were sure: No Tongue had penetrated the Apache camp in the most daring manner, and had set them free at the risk of his own life.

He had disappeared now, but they felt abundantly able to look out for themselves.

Even the ordinary watchers of the corral had left their stations to join the shouting crowd in camp, who were boasting of their victory, and the escaping Lipans could do about as they pleased.

They could find no weapons, but there were saddles and bridles, and scores and scores of fleet steeds to choose from, and it was but a few minutes before Two Knives and his friends were leading their selections through the darkness toward the river. They did not hunt for any ford. Horses and men alike knew how to swim. Once safely across, there was a great temptation to give a whoop, but the chief forbade it.

"No. Keep still. No Tongue is on the trail of the Apaches. Noise bad for him."

With that he sprung into his saddle, and led the way at a fierce gallop. If their horses should not fall with them and break their necks they would soon be beyond pursuit. It was a somewhat reckless thing to do, considering how many squads of Apaches were on that prairie, but they had no weapons, not so much as a knife, among them, and speed seemed to be their only hope.

William O. Stoddard

CHAPTER XXV

All the ordinary rules and regulations for the government of an Indian village were knocked in pieces by the arrival of such an event as the victory over the Lipans.

Even Mother Dolores could not reasonably have forbidden Ni-ha-be and Rita from hurrying out of their lodge to join in the general rejoicing. In fact, Dolores had left them to their own devices a full minute before they made their appearance.

"Rita, there is Knotted Cord!"

"I see him."

"If he could understand me I would speak to him."

"Oh, Ni-ha-be! That would be a dreadful thing to do."

Ni-ha-be would not have done any such thing, and Rita knew it; but the chief's daughter saw no reason why she should not lead her sister pretty near the young pale-face brave as they passed him. They could see that he was smiling at them, and it was an act of politeness to smile back. Ni-ha-be laughed.

It was that, perhaps, which led Steve into a mistake. He

wanted to say something, and in his haste he forgot to speak Mexican Spanish, as he ought to have done, if he expected to be understood by an Apache young lady.

"There has been a great fight. Your father has taken some prisoners."

"We know it," answered Rita, and she was almost as much startled as was Steve himself.

"What! Do you understand English?"

Ni-ha-be turned at the same moment, and looked at her in astonishment.

"Only some. A little. Not any more talk now. Come, Ni-ha-be."

"Talk Apache, so I can hear. You shall not say any more words to him. Tell me what you said. Tell me his words."

Ni-ha-be's jealous pride was touched to the quick at finding that Rita possessed still another accomplishment that she had not. It was worse than even the talking leaves, for Rita had not seemed to hear them very well. It was too bad!

Rita quickly interpreted all that had been said, but she did it in a way that told both her sister and Steve Harrison that she was a good deal excited about something.

"Come, Ni-ha-be, come."

"I will. There is Red Wolf. We must hurry."

Poor Rita! The whooping and clamor and tumult and confusion all around her confused her more than ever. She was glad there was enough of it to keep Ni-ha-be from asking her any questions; but it seemed as if she would be willing to give her favorite pony to hear a few words more in that strange tongue—the tongue she had known once, and forgotten, till the talking leaves began to speak it to her.

Pretty soon the girls were mingling with their friends and relations, crowding as closely as they dared upon the line of warriors, and striving to get a glimpse of the prisoners by the light of the camp-fires.

It was getting late, but Many Bears had work to do before he could think of calling for a luncheon or going to his lodge. He had seen his captives safely bound and put away under guard, and he now summoned his old men for a brief but very important "talk."

Murray had guessed right when he said he would be sent for, but he had not waited the arrival of any messenger. The words were hardly out of the mouth of Many Bears before a brave in the crowd responded,

"Send Warning is here."

"Where is the Knotted Cord?"

"In lodge. Wait there."

That explanation came from Red Wolf, and the Apaches knew exactly where their pale-face friends were at that particular moment, which was the precise thing Murray wanted them to feel sure of, considering what he knew was about to be found out.

All the rest of the village was full of noise, but the dignity of the older men enforced silence in the circle now gathering closely around the chief. Added to the dignity was a large amount of pride over what they had already done, and a little anxiety concerning what it would be best to do next.

Many Bears turned to Murray. "Send Warning gave good council. His head is white. He is wise. Tell Apaches now where all pale-face gone. No come."

"Send Warning can guess. The pale-faces don't like to be killed. Find too many Apaches. Run away and save scalp."

"Ugh! Good. Nobody know where they go. No use follow. Apaches take Lipan prisoners. What Send Warning say about them?"

"Keep them till to-morrow. No hurry. Something else to think of now. More fight, maybe."

The chief nodded his head, but a chorus of "Ughs!" expressed the dissent of his council. They meant to decide the fate of old Two Knives without delay.

Still, three of the older braves insisted upon arguing the case, one after the other; and by the time the last of them ceased speaking, Murray felt pretty safe about To-la-go-to-de. He said to himself, "The old fox has half an hour the start of them now. He is miles and miles away."

Just then Many Bears turned to him with, "What say now? Any words?"

"No. Never speak twice. Apaches do what think best."

"Ugh! Good. Young braves bring out Lipans. No wait. Kill them all right away."

William O. Stoddard

Prisoners of such a sort were likely to be a troublesome burden to a party on the march like that of Many Bears, and the only real question before the council was, after all, in what precise manner the killing should be done.

At that moment, however, a great cry arose from the vicinity of the lodge where the Lipans had been shut up—a cry of surprise, anger, and disappointment. And then the word spread over the whole camp like wildfire,

"The Lipans are gone!"

It was almost beyond belief, and there was a general rush toward that row of lodges, and beyond them into the bushes and through the corral. It came within an ace of stampeding every pony there, and every trace of anything like a "trail" left by the feet of Two Knives and his warriors was quickly trampled out.

The only bit of a "sign" found by anybody was in the shape of more than a dozen thongs of buckskin on the ground in the lodge, all clean cut through with a sharp knife.

That told plainly how the prisoners had released themselves.

The braves who had searched and tied them were positive that not one of them retained a knife, or was left in a condition to make any use of one. They must have had help from somebody, but it was a great mystery who that somebody could be.

Suspicion might have fallen upon Murray and Steve, but it was well known that the latter had remained in his lodge, refusing even to look at the prisoners, while Send Warning had been in council with the chiefs. They believed they knew where he had been all the while, and none of them imagined that Two Knives had been set free before he had lain in that "prison lodge" three minutes.

It was a terrible mortification, but something must be done; and again Murray was asked for advice.

"What do I think? Let me ask you a question. Did the Lipans go away on foot?"

"Ugh! No. Take good horse."

"Did they have any arms? Gun? lance? bow?"

"Ugh! No. Think not."

"They are cunning warriors. Did they ride out among your young men? Send Warning says they would do just what great Apache chief would do."

"Ugh! Good. Pale-face chief very wise. Lipans go all way round. Like snake. Only one thing for us to do. Catch 'em when they come to pass."

"Better ride now," said Murray. "Send Warning and Knotted Cord will ride with Apache braves. No time lose. Want fresh horse."

He afterward explained to Steve that a little seeming activity on their part was needful at that moment of excitement, lest anything unpleasant should be said about them. Besides, he had no fear of any farther collision with the Lipans. The night was too far gone for that, and he had great confidence in the courage and skill of old Two Knives.

In less than twenty minutes after he had given his advice, he and Steve Harrison, mounted on fresh mustangs chosen for them from the corral by Red Wolf himself, were riding across the ford at the head of a strong squad of Apache warriors, commanded by a chief of well-known skill and prowess.

"They will pick up plenty more on the way, Steve, but they won't have much to do."

"No danger of their catching old Two Knives?"

"Not a bit. I'll tell you all about it some other time."

"I've something to tell you, Murray. I can't keep it."

"Out with it, my boy."

"That white daughter of old Many Bears can speak English. She understood what I said and answered me."

It was dark, or Steve would have seen that the face of his friend grew as white as his hair, and then flushed and brightened with a great and sudden light.

For a moment he was silent, and then he said, in a deep, husky voice,

"Don't say any more about it to me, Steve. Not till I speak to you again. I'm in an awful state of mind to-night."

Steve had somehow made up his mind to that already, but he was saved the necessity of saying anything in reply. Red Wolf rode closer to him at the moment and said,

"Knotted Cord is young. Been on war-path before?"

"Say yes, Steve," muttered Murray.

"Yes, I'm young. Seen a good deal, though. Many war-paths."

"What tribe strike?"

"Lipans, Comanches, Mexicans. Followed some Pawnees once. They got away."

Red Wolf's whole manner told of the respect he felt for a young brave who had already been out against the fiercest warriors of the Indian country. He would have given a good many ponies to have been able to say as much for himself.

"Glad come among Apaches. Stay long time. Never go away."

That was a wonderful thing for Red Wolf to say, considering what a bitter prejudice had been taught him against everybody with a white skin. Ni-ha-be would not have believed it unless she had heard him say it.

"Can't promise," replied Steve. "Go when Send Warning say."

No comment could be made by a "young brave" on an appeal to a white-headed "chief" like Murray, and the talk slackened a little.

It would hardly have done so if they could have looked a few miles in front of them just then. The darkness would have prevented their seeing much, but if they had been near the old Lipan camp they would have seen that it was empty.

A few Apaches had taken possession of it at first, but the smouldering camp-fires and blazing wagons gave light enough to the Lipans among the rocks to enable them to send occasional bullets at whatever might be stirring there, and the place was given up as uselessly dangerous. The scattered shots which now and then came from the mouth of the pass told that the beaten warriors of To-la-go-to-de were wide-awake and ready to defend themselves, and their position was well known to be a strong one—not to be attacked without both orders and re-enforcements.

But for one thing that end of the pass would have been already vacant. The pride of the Lipans forbade their running farther without at least an effort to learn what had become of their chief. They felt that they could never look their squaws in the face again unless they could explain that point.

To be sure it was almost a hopeless case, and the Apaches would be upon them in the morning, but they waited.

Everything seemed to be growing darker, and the outlying Lipan sentinels were not in any fault that four men on horseback should get so near them undiscovered. It was very near, and the new-comers must have known there was danger in it, for one of them suddenly put his hand to his mouth and uttered a fierce, half-triumphant war-whoop. It was the well-known battle-cry of To-la-go-to-de himself, and it was answered by a storm of exulting shouts from the warriors among the rocks. Their chief had escaped!

That was true, and it was a grand thing, but he had brought back with him only three men of his "front rank."

The Apaches could hear the whooping, and the foremost of them deemed it wise to fall back a little. Whatever their enemies might be up to, they were men to be watched with prudence as well as courage.

The words of the great chief were few. There was no farther account to be made of Captain Skinner and his miners, he told them. They were cunning, and they had taken care of themselves. It had been well to plunder their camp. He himself owed his safety to their old friend No Tongue, and the Lipans must never forget him. The Yellow Head had probably been killed, and they would not see him again. They must now gather all their horses and other plunder, and push their retreat as far as possible before morning. Some other time they would come and strike the Apaches, but it was "bad medicine" for them just now.

Whatever else that may have meant, according to Indian superstition, every warrior could understand that their losses had weakened them too much to think of fighting another hard battle. It was no disgrace to make a great deal of haste under such circumstances; and so, if Red Wolf and the rest had been near enough at that hour, they would have seen Two Knives and what was left of his band riding steadily on, deeper and deeper, among the mountains.

William O. Stoddard

CHAPTER XXVI

All the while that Murray had been sitting among the Apache chiefs and answering their questions, and even when he and Steve mounted the mustangs Red Wolf brought them, there had been three pairs of very keen eyes, not to speak of any others, closely watching him.

"He is not an Apache!" exclaimed Ni-ha-be to Rita. "Why do they make a chief of him? He is nothing but an old pale-face!"

"He is wise. He is good. The great chief listens to him. All the warriors listen. They did as he said to-night, and so they beat the Lipans."

"He is not a warrior. He did not go out and fight."

"All warriors do not go always. Some stay in camp. Young squaws like you and me must not talk about chiefs."

That was good Apache teaching, and Ni-ha-be knew it, but she seemed to have formed a strong dislike for Send Warning, and she retorted,

"He is not a chief—only a pale-face. I will talk about him as much as I please. You like him because he is one of your own people."

Rita was silent. There was a very strange feeling in her heart just then, and she was trying to understand it.

For long years, ever since she was a little girl, she had been taught to think of herself as an Apache maiden, the daughter of a great chief, and she had grown to be very proud of it. She had been even ashamed, at times, of the fact that, in some way that she did not quite understand, she was a pale-face also. Ni-ha-be had been apt to throw it at her whenever there was any dispute between them, and that had helped to keep her from forgetting it.

And, now she had seen Send Warning and Knotted Cord, she had felt that a sort of change was coming over her. She was young, but she could see that in some way they were the superiors of all the red warriors around them. They were listened to and looked up to, although they were almost strangers. To her eyes they were better-looking, something higher and nobler, and she was not at all ashamed of the thought that they belonged to her own people. Then it had come to her, with a great rush of joy in her heart, that she could speak her own language—a little of it. She could even hear many words from the mysterious talking leaves of the pale-faces, and no Apache girl could do that—not even Ni-ha-be herself, for all her wonderfully good eyes.

Then there came to the camp the great excitement caused by finding out the escape of the Lipan prisoners, and quickly after that had come the departure of the force sent out to recapture them.

Rita and Ni-ha-be had been standing side by side, watching all that was done.

"Send Warning is going on the war-path now, Ni-ha-be."

"So are Red Wolf and Knotted Cord. Young braves are worth more than wrinkled old men."

"The great chief himself is wrinkled a little."

"He is a great brave. He must be angry by this time. He will send for Dolores."

They did not know how earnestly that important woman had been using her own eyes all that time. She had seen as much as had either of them, and she was close to them at that moment.

"Young squaws go back to lodge right away. See? All squaws go in a hurry."

A few sharp words from one of the old men had started them, and they were indeed hurrying. They knew there was a good deal of bad temper up in the village just then, and there was no telling who might be made to suffer for it. The last squaw to get home would be very likely to meet a cross husband, and Indian husbands are not pleasant company when anything has made them cross.

The two girls hurried with the rest, and Dolores had very little to say to them.

It was now Ni-ha-be's turn to notice something of a change. Not in herself, but in Dolores. She had been accustomed to feel that whatever difference was made between Rita and herself was in her own favor. She felt that it was right it should be so, much as she loved her adopted sister, for after all it was a great advantage to be every bit an Apache. She was often sorry for Rita, but she could not help her having been born white.

Now, however, although it required all her keenness to detect it, there seemed to be something of unusual respect in the voice and manner of Dolores whenever she spoke to Rita. A touch of special kindness came with it. Not a sign of harshness showed itself all the way to the lodge, although Dolores had one or two pretty sharp things to say to Ni-ha-be. The Mexican darkness of the chief's "great cook" had helped everybody to almost forget her origin, but the thought of it came slowly into Ni-ha-be's mind.

"She read one of the talking leaves herself. It made her shut her eyes and kneel down. Send Warning talked with her. She is as bad as Rita. She is not an Apache at heart."

That was hardly fair to Mother Dolores, for it was only too true that, as Murray said of her, "she was completely Indianized." Even now she was not thinking of herself as a pale-face, or longing to be anything else than the "cook squaw" of the mighty war-chief Many Bears. No; she was not thinking of herself, but a great cloud was gathering in her mind, and she felt that it all belonged in some way to Rita.

She did not speak of it, but she felt a good deal more comfortable after the two girls were safe behind the skin cover of their own lodge.

"Great chief not go on war-path. Better not see young squaws just now. He will send for the talking leaves in the morning. Send Warning will read them to him. He did not look so old to-night. He was a very handsome man when he was young. So long ago!"

Ni-ha-be had been right about her father's appetite, for it was only a few minutes before he came stalking toward the camp-fire for some venison-steak, and Dolores had been wise enough to have it on the coals, so as not to keep him waiting.

He never dreamed of telling her, nor she of asking him, anything about the events of the night or the plans of the warriors, but all the while that steak was broiling she was thinking of Send Warning rather than of Many Bears, and wondering if there would be another fight with the Lipans before sunrise. That was the very question asked of Murray by the chief in command of their squad half an hour or so later.

"What do I think? Well, I think the Lipans are not fools."

"What mean by that?"

"Fools stay and get killed. Cunning men ride hard and get away."

The Apaches rode a little faster after that, and were joined by so many other small parties of warriors that they were quite a respectable force by the time they reached the neighborhood of the camp. It was nearly sunrise then, and the braves who had been watching the camp faithfully reported all that had occurred. They told of the sudden whooping nearly two hours earlier, and Murray at once remarked, "Apache chief knows what that means?"

"He is not very wise. Send Warning tell him."

"It meant that their great chief and the three braves with him had come back to them. Send warrior up toward pass. If I am wrong, the Lipans are there now; if I am right, they are gone."

The warrior scout was sent in a twinkling, for Indian sagacity understood the keenness of Murray's guess, and it was not long before the news came back that not a sign of an enemy could be discovered among the rocks.

It was a disappointment. The daring invaders had escaped, for there would be no use in following them. The whole Apache nation could hardly have forced the narrow places of that pass against so strong a party of good rifle-men. Neither was there any certainty but what the pale-face miners might be in there somewhere, ready to deal destruction on any Apache who should be so unwise as to ride into such a rocky trap.

The sun arose while they were talking about it, and the Apache braves were already searching the camp for anything which might have been left.

They were not without some success, for the first wagon had not burnt very well, and the Lipans had neither time nor heart to take everything out of it.

"Come, Steve. The miners made their last camp over yonder. I can see a wagon-wheel sticking up."

A quick gallop brought them to all that was left of that second wagon. It had burnt better than the other, but had not been completely consumed.

"Nothing left in it."

"If there had been, the Apaches would be here now instead of over yonder. I declare!"

He sprung from his pony, and rushed toward the one hind-wheel which was still upheld by what was left of its broken axle, and by a part of the wagon bottom.

"What is it, Murray?"

"Wait a moment."

Steve too was on foot, just as the old man gave that wheel a jerk that dragged it several feet from its place.

"Look there, Steve!"

"Buckskin bags—some of them half burnt. What is that, Murray, in the ashes? Is it gold?"

"More than that, Steve. It's gold coin—twenty-dollar gold pieces. Stow away as many of those little bags as you can before any Apaches come. It's our plunder."

"They're coming. But how is it ours?"

He was picking up several of the little bags, and putting them inside his hunting-shirt when he asked that question.

"Because we're on this war-path, and have found it. The Apaches would rather have ponies; but they may take what we leave, if they want it."

"Doesn't it belong to those miners? Won't they come for it?"

"They would not find it if they did come, but they never will. They'll trust the Apaches and Lipans too well for that. Besides, it never was theirs. They stole every cent of it."

"Do you suppose we can ever find the owners?"

"Never. It would be an utter impossibility. What we are

picking up is ours, by all the laws of the mountains and all the rules of Indian war."

They did not open a single one of the little buckskin bags, but Murray threw down one that would not "chink" and picked up another.

"Coin is better than dust or nuggets, Steve, and we must not take it all. Only what we can stow away quickly. It's just what we are going to need. It will pay the expenses of your trip to the settlements, and take care of you after you get there."

His face was burning hot while he spoke, and his eyes were flashing with sudden and fierce excitement. Could it be possible that he was so terribly fond of money?

Steve wondered and stared, but the Apache young men were crowding around them now, and Murray nodded to him to fall back.

"Mount at once, Steve. Don't seem to claim anything or to interfere. Let them sift the ashes if they want to."

"Seems to me we must have the best part of it."

"That's likely. I think we have as much as we shall need. No. I don't know how much I may need before I get through. Money is a good thing to have sometimes."

Murray was hardly himself that morning, and yet he met the Apache leader coolly enough.

"What do now? Send Warning advise friend."

"Ride back to village. Not lose time. Young men finish

plunder. Old men not stay. Great chief want to see us."

That last word was enough and the warrior wheeled his horse westward. His parting orders were few, but they would bring back every Apache from that "war-path" as soon as the search for plunder should be completed.

"It's all right, Steve," said Murray, as they rode along side by side. "If we had stayed there too long some of them might have been curious how much we had picked up. They won't say a word after we are in camp. If an Indian once gets his plunder safe into his own lodge nobody questions his title to it. That is, if it has been taken from an enemy."

CHAPTER XXVII

Not one of the persons who had "wondered what had become of those miners" had so much as guessed at the exact truth, although Murray had come nearer to it than anybody else.

That sunrise found them, as they thought, once for all safe within the boundary of the "foreign country," where no one would ask them any ugly questions about the stolen gold they had brought there.

In fact, the first thing they did, after finishing their hearty breakfast of fresh beef, was to "unpack themselves." Every man wanted to know if he had lost anything on the way, and to make as good a guess as he could how much his load was worth. Then it seemed as if they all spoke together when they tried to express their regret at having been compelled to leave any of their treasure behind.

"No use to think of going back for it now, boys. Some day we'll take another look at that mine, but there won't be a thing worth going for in that wagon."

"What do ye mean to do next, Cap?" asked Bill.

"I told you before. Give our horses a chance to feed, and then push right on. We can afford to use 'em all up now. Three days of hard riding'll carry us out of harm's way."

"And then we can go jest whar we please."

There was a wonderful deal of comfort in that for men who had been "running away" so long as they had, and over so very rough a country. Their hard, rude, weather-beaten faces began to put on an expression of peace and quiet, and even of good-nature, and they gave their weary horses a longer rest than they had at first intended. After that, however, the sharp, stern summons of Captain Skinner called them to "mount and ride" once more, and they were all ready to obey. It was a wild region through which they were going, but at more than one place they passed the ruins of old houses and other traces of former attempts at settlement and cultivation.

"There were good ranches hereaway in the old times," said Captain Skinner, "and there was some mining done, but it was too near the Apache range, and there were too many revolutions. It won't be settled up till there's a new state of things. The Apaches'll take care of that."

All their troubles, they thought, were behind them, and they cared very little for those of the country they had gotten into— less than they might have done if they had imagined how nearly those very troubles might yet concern themselves.

It was impossible, however, not to think and talk about the Apaches, and to "wonder how the Lipans came out of their attack on that village."

Captain Skinner's comment was, "I don't reckon a great many of 'em came out at all. The chances were against them. Old Two Knives made a mistake for once, and I shouldn't wonder if he'd had to pay for it."

Well, so he had, but not so heavily as the Captain imagined.

At that very moment he was leading through the homeward pass just about half of his original war-party—all that "had come out of the attack on that village."

The village itself was in a high state of fermentation that morning. There was mourning in some of the lodges over braves who had fallen in that brief, sharp battle with the Lipans, but there were only five of these in all, so great had been the advantage of superior numbers in the fight, and of holding the ground of it afterward.

The bitterest disgrace of To-la-go-to-de and his warriors had been their failure to carry off the bodies of their friends who had fallen. At least twenty of the Apaches had been more or less wounded, and every man of them was as proud of it as if he had been "promoted." A scar received in battle is a badge of honor to an Indian warrior, and he is apt to make a show of it on every fair opportunity.

There was no need, therefore, of throwing away any pity on those who had been cut by the lances or "barked" by the bullets of the Lipans. Red Wolf himself had concealed a smart score of a lance-thrust along his left side, for fear he might be forbidden going on that second war-path. Even now he refused to consider it as amounting to anything, and his sister's face glowed with family pride as she said to Rita,

"Red Wolf is a true Apache. He's a warrior already. He will be a great chief some day. The Knotted Cord is white. He has no scars. He has never been on a war-path."

She was speaking in her brother's hearing, and Steve was at no great distance at that very moment, talking, in a low, earnest tone, with Murray.

Rita replied, "He is young. Send Warning is a warrior—" But Red Wolf broke in, very honestly, with,

"Knotted Cord is my brother. Only his skin is white. Not his heart. He is a warrior. He has been on war-paths. He has seen the Lipans, the Comanches, the Pawnees, the Mexicans. He is not a boy."

Ni-ha-be's little "pet" was blown away by that, and she looked once more admiringly at the strong and handsome young pale-face. If he had only been so fortunate as to be born an Apache, what might not have been expected of him!

The girls had many questions to ask concerning the events of the night before, and Red Wolf was in an accommodating frame of mind that morning. It was right, too, in his opinion, that the squaws of his family should be able to boast among the other squaws of the mighty doings of their father and brother. That was the way the reputations of warriors were to be made and kept up, aided now and then by the good things they might see fit to say about themselves.

In all that there is just this difference between red men and white, and it would soon disappear with civilization.

That is, when a great white "brave" of any kind does a thing he is proud of he manages to have the story of it printed in the newspapers, so that all his boasting is done for him by somebody else.

The Indian "brave" is compelled to be his own newspaper, and tell his own story of himself. That is all, and it sometimes makes the poor red man appear to be the vainer of the two, which is a great injustice.

The conversation between Steve and Murray could not be

overheard by their friends, but it must have been of more than a little importance, to judge by the expression that came and went upon their faces. No Indian warrior's face would have betrayed his feelings in such a manner.

Dolores was busy at the camp-fires, as usual, with her frying-pan, and they were looking at her.

"How old do you think she is, Steve?"

"It's hard to guess, Murray. Maybe she's forty-five."

"She is not much above thirty. The Mexican women grow old sooner than white ones. She was not much above twenty when she cooked for my miners on the Santa Rita mine."

"Do you feel perfectly sure about that?"

"I've watched her. There is no doubt left in my mind. Still, I may ask her a few more questions. Then there is one thing more I want to make sure of."

"Will it keep us here long?"

"It may keep me, Steve."

"Then it will keep me, Murray. You will need me if you have anything on hand. I am anxious enough to get off, but I will not leave you behind. I'll stay and help."

Murray held out his hand.

"It's a fact, Steve. I may need all the help you can give."

"Take care! Here comes Many Bears himself, and two of his cunningest councillors."

It did not require much guessing on Steve's part to know that, for the "cunning" of those old Indians was written all over their dark, wrinkled faces.

"More advice wanted," thought Murray, but it was not asked for so soon as he expected.

The first words of Many Bears were complimentary, of course. His pale-face friend had been very wise. All he had said had been good, even to the not permitting the young men to follow the Lipans into the mountains. Warriors had told the chief that Send Warning and Knotted Cord had picked up something in the camp of the pale-faces. The Apaches were glad. Their friends were welcome to what they had found. Murray interrupted him there by promptly holding out one of the little buckskin bags.

"Great chief take it."

"No. No want it. Send Warning keep it, and tell Apaches what better do next."

"Go to better hunting-ground. Bad place for camp."

"Will the Lipans come again?"

"Not till after next snow. Got enough now. Come then."

All that and more came in as a sort of preface to what Many Bears really wanted to say. He had something very heavy on his mind that morning, and in order to get rid of it he had to tell the whole story of the buffalo-hunt his band had made away beyond the mountains into the country claimed by the Lipans. That was the way they came to be followed so closely by Two Knives and his warriors.

Murray and Steve listened closely, for the chief spoke in very good Mexican Spanish most of the time, and they both understood him. Then came the story of the return through the pass, and it wound up with the finding of the talking leaves by Rita.

"Send Warning knows the rest."

"No," said Murray, "I have not seen the talking leaves."

"Great medicine. Tell Apache chief about miners. Tell about old fight. Tell about blue-coat soldiers come, and where go. Tell about big talk, and treaty, and presents. Many Bears want to hear more."

"Ask young squaw."

"Can't hear all. Send Warning listen. Say what he hears."

"All right. Bring young squaw."

"No need of squaw. Bring talking leaves."

"No," persisted Murray. "Young squaw find. All her medicine. Must hold leaves for Send Warning to read."

"Ugh! Good. Many Bears not care. Dolores bring Rita. Tell her to bring leaves."

Ni-ha-be and Rita were near enough to hear, and the latter at once darted into the lodge for her treasures, while her adopted sister looked after her with a good deal of envy in her eyes.

"She is a pale-face. It is too bad."

Rita was gone but a moment, and her whole body seemed to glow and tremble with excitement as she held out the three magazines to Murray.

"Take one, Steve. You haven't forgotten your reading, have you?"

"Send Warning hear leaves," said Many Bears, anxiously. "The Knotted Cord is young."

"He is white. He can hear. The great chief will listen."

"Ugh!" muttered Ni-ha-be, looking on from a little distance, but Rita looked at Steve, with a bright smile on her face.

"There, Murray," said Steve, "the chief was right. There's a picture of cavalry. All the others he spoke of are here. Here is the picture of the big talk and the treaty."

"Here is the mining fight—" and just there Murray paused as if he could say no more, and the Indians looked at him in undisguised astonishment. His breast was heaving, his lips were quivering, and the hands that held the magazines were trembling as if their owner had an ague fit.

"What find?" exclaimed Many Bears. "Is it bad medicine?"

It was some seconds before Murray could trust himself to speak, but he was thinking very fast.

"The talking leaves have told Many Bears the truth. Now Send Warning is troubled in his mind."

All could see that, and it made them not a little anxious.

"What want? What do?"

"Go into lodge with young squaw. Knotted Cord stay and talk with Apache chief. Nobody come into lodge. Take a little time. Then tell what hear."

It was an unusual request, but there could be no objection, in view of the fact that there was "great medicine" to be looked into. An Indian conjurer always requires the absence of all observers for the performance of his most important juggling. It was at once decided by the chief that Send Warning should have his way.

Rita listened, pale and serious, while Ni-ha-be looked on in jealous amazement.

"I am an Apache girl? Why can he not teach me to hear the talking leaves?"

No doubt he could have done so if she would have given him plenty of time, and been willing to begin with A B C, as Rita had done long years before.

How should all that ABC business have come back to Rita as it did, when she found herself alone in her lodge with that white-headed old pale-face warrior?

She thought she had never before seen so kind and good a face, and she wondered that it did not seem so very old, after all, now it was so near.

"I will sit down, Rita, my dear. Sit down too. You are too tall now to stand up."

Not a human eye was looking upon them, but Rita had suddenly covered her face with her hands.

"Speak," she said, earnestly; "I remember better when I do

not see."

She was talking English, just as he had done, only more slowly, and almost as if it hurt her.

"I will read the first word, dear. Then you may spell it. M-i-n-e, mine. That means a gold-mine, like ours, dear. Spell it, Rita, my darling."

"Our mine? Darling? Oh, if I could see my father!"

Murray sprung to his feet as if he were a boy. His mouth opened and closed as if he were keeping back a great shout, and the tears came pouring down over his cheeks.

"Rita! Rita! My dear little daughter! Here I am!"

"Father!"

His arms were around her now, and he was kissing her almost frantically.

Slowly she opened her eyes. "I know it is you when you speak, and when my eyes are shut. When I open them you are very old. My father was young and handsome. His hair was not white."

"Rita, darling, it has been just as white as it is now ever since the morning after I came home and found that the Apaches had carried you away. They killed your mother, and I heard that they had killed you too. I have been an old man ever since, but I think I shall grow young again now."

Time was precious. They could only spare enough for a few hurried questions and answers, and Murray glanced rapidly over the pages of the three magazines.

"Let me take them," he said. "I would like to read them carefully. I shall know what to say to the chief. You must not let anybody know I am your father—not till the right time comes."

"Oh, why not?"

"Because the Apaches would know then that I am their enemy, and have good reason to be. Even if they did not kill me at once, they would not trust me, and I want them to do that. It is my only hope of carrying you away with me. Stay here in the lodge till you are sure your face will not betray you."

She had been crying more copiously than her father, and that would have been a thing to be explained to Ni-ha-be and Dolores. Rita therefore remained in the lodge while Murray, with a great effort, recovered his usual calm self-control, and walked slowly and dignifiedly out. He needed to put on all the dignity he was master of, for his heart was thump-thumping against his ribs, and his brain was in a whirl as to when and how he should be able to claim and carry on the great treasure he had found.

Treasure! The Buckhorn Mine, piled mountain high with twenty-dollar pieces, was nothing to it.

William O. Stoddard

CHAPTER XXVIII

Steve Harrison found his position a little awkward during the time spent by Murray with Rita in the lodge. The chiefs had too much dignity to seem to consult with so young a brave especially as he had not even one of the talking leaves to listen to. He knew that not only Dolores and Ni-ha-be, but half a dozen other squaws, old and young, were staring at him, and he could not understand a word of the low-voiced remarks they made. He was very glad, therefore, when his friend once more appeared, and he saw by the light on his face that he had no unpleasant news to bring.

"What find?" asked Many Bears. "Send Warning and Rita hear something?"

"Hear a little. Send Warning will take the leaves to his own lodge and hear more."

"What say now? Hear about big talk with blue-coat pale-faces?"

"Tell you what I think."

"The chief is listening."

"Break up village. Move west right away. More news come

soon. Hear about treaty when you see the lodges of your own people. No time to lose."

That advice agreed so exactly with the notions of Many Bears that he was ready to accept it at once. He turned to his two councillors triumphantly.

"What did I tell you? It is wisdom. We will go. Tell the braves to get ready. Tell all the squaws to pack up. Send on hunting braves. Good many. Kill plenty meat."

There was no opposition. The only objection that could reasonably be raised was that so sudden a departure gave no opportunity for a grand celebration of their victory over the Lipans. They could attend to that some other time, and there was no doubt but what all the whooping and boasting in the band would keep safely till it should be called for.

"Come, Steve," said Murray. "We want an hour by ourselves."

They were quickly inside their own lodge, and were sure there were no listeners.

"Steve!"

"What is it, Murray?"

"That little girl is my own daughter!"

"I've suspected it. And this was the very band of Apaches that broke up your home and your mine."

"Yes, and it is a wonder they have not recognized me. If Apaches of some other band were to join them, some of them might remember me. They have seen me in more than one of their fights with the Lipans."

"It would be all over with us then."

"Of course it would. I am dressed differently, to be sure. I can change a little more. Must crop my hair and beard closer. They know me for a long-bearded old man. I must turn myself into a short-haired young one."

"Can't you dye your hair?"

"Not till we get to the settlements. There are no barbers among the Apaches."

"How will we ever get her away, Murray?"

"Oh, my girl! My poor, dear little girl! I dare not think about my wife. No wonder my hair is white. Steve, I must not let her live and die among these wild people. They have been kind to her, she says; and I do not hate them so much now I know that, but she shall not be an Indian."

He was getting feverishly excited, and Steve replied,

"Now, Murray, of course we will get her away. Haven't you some plan?"

"Only to draw the whole band nearer the frontier, or nearer to some fort or other."

"That's good. We should have a shorter distance to run, if we should escape."

"Now, Steve, I'm all upset and unstrung. That's the reason I came in here. I've got to get my wits about me again, or I can't plan anything."

"Sit down and read."

"Read? Do you suppose I could do that just now? Why, Steve, I've found my little daughter!"

"So you have. I don't wonder you're excited. I am myself. Here, give me a magazine. I'd like to find out how much of my reading will come back."

Murray handed him one, and Steve sat down. He had been fond of books in the days before he was captured by the Lipans. He had not forgotten his reading at all, and it came back to him in a way that made his heart jump. But that was after he had made a great effort, and driven away the faces of Rita and Ni-ha-be.

Both of them would somehow come between his eyes and the paper of those printed pages at first. Both of them were such nice, pretty, well-behaved girls, and yet one of them was white, the daughter of his friend Murray, and the other was only a poor little squaw of the Apaches.

How the black eyes of Ni-ha-be would have snapped if she could have read the thoughts of Knotted Cord at that moment! She would never again have regarded him as a handsome young brave, almost good enough to be an Apache.

Murray, too, picked up a magazine and sat down.

"It will do for a sort of medicine," he muttered. "I may learn something from it, too. The world has changed a great deal since I have had newspapers or magazines to read. There may be some new nations in it, for all I know, and there surely must be a new lot of kings and queens and presidents, and all that sort of thing."

William O. Stoddard

It was that thought which made him turn over a little carelessly all the illustrated articles and the stories, till he came to the "news of the month" among the leaves at the end.

There he began actually to read, and read closely, for it was all very new to him, although it was several months since it had been printed there.

There was a great deal of it, for the editor had condensed everything into the fewest words possible, and more than once Murray's eyes opened wider or his mouth puckered up as if for a whistle. The world had been moving fast while he had been among the Lipans.

"And Rita," he muttered, "she knows nothing at all about any of it. I don't know that I am sorry. She will have all the pleasure of learning all she needs to know, and she won't have anything to unlearn. I wish I could forget some things as completely as she seems to have done. I hope a good many of them will never come back to her at all."

No doubt it was very interesting, and Steve looked up from his own reading to see how completely absorbed Murray had become.

Still, it must have been a remarkable news item that could make a man of steady nerves bound suddenly to his feet and hold that magazine out at arm's length.

"Why, Murray," said Steve, "what can be the matter?"

"Matter? My dear boy! Read that! Rita is an heiress."

"What?"

He might well have been half afraid his friend had lost his wits, but he took the "talking leaves" held out to him, and read the few lines to which the finger of Murray was pointing:

"The great English estate of Cranston Hall, with a baronetcy, is waiting for an heir. The late baronet left no children, and his only brother, to whom the title and all descend, was last heard of in America. He is believed to have been interested in mining in the Far West, and the lawyers are hunting for him."

"Well," said Murray, when Steve ceased reading, "what do you think of that?"

"I don't know exactly what to think. Your name is Murray."

"Robert Cranston Murray, as my father's was before me. It was because he left me only my name that I left England to seek my fortune. Oh, Steve! I must find my way back now. Rita will be the lady of Cranston Hall!"

"Instead of the squaw of some Apache horse-stealer!"

Steve felt a little like dancing, and a good deal like tossing up his hat and venting his feelings by a good hurrah, but the next thought was a sober one.

"How are we ever to get them to give up Rita?"

Murray was thinking the same thought just then, and it seemed to him as if he must go out to the door of the lodge for a little breath of fresh air.

The chief and his councillors were nowhere to be seen, but there was Mother Dolores by the camp-fire.

William O. Stoddard

Murray tried hard to assume a calm and steady face and voice as he strode forward and stood beside her. He spoke to her in Spanish.

"Well, Dolores, which do you like best, cooking for Mexican miners or for the great chief?"

She dropped her stew-pan and stood looking at him for a moment, drawing her breath hard, and then she exclaimed,

"I was right. It is Senor Murray. Ah, senor, it is so long ago! The poor senora—"

"Don't speak of her. I know. We found her. My Rita?"

"Yes, she is your Rita. But they will kill you if you tell them. I will keep your secret, senor. I have kept it now."

She had dimly recognized him, then, and she, too, had been in doubt what to do or say. In answer to a few more questions she told him very truly that she had been better off among the Apaches than before she was captured. Less hard work, better treatment, better food, better position, just about as much real civilization.

Poor Dolores had never known much about that or anything better than the hard lot of a Mexican woman of the lower class among the rough miners. It was better, she said, to be the wife of a chief and have plenty to eat, and little hard work to do.

"But about Rita?"

"If you had your mine now, and your great droves of horses!"

"What could I do?"

"Do, Senor Murray? Why, you could buy half the young squaws in the village, if you had husbands for them. But you are poor now. I suppose it cannot be done."

It was no wonder he had not thought of it before. It was so strange a thing to propose. That a father should buy his own daughter! He turned from her and strode back to his own lodge, to hear what Steve would say. "He's a mere boy, but sometimes he seems to have a great deal of sense."

Steve's remark, after he had heard about Dolores and her idea, was simply,

"That's nothing new, is it? If we can't run away with her, we can ransom her."

"Ransom? Well, now, that's a great deal better word than buy. But our gold coin won't do. They won't take the whole pile for her. They don't really understand the value of it."

"They want ponies, and blankets, and all that?"

"That's it. Why, Steve, it's the queerest thing. I'm so excited I can't think. If we can make a bargain with them they'll be glad enough to go with us to the nearest trading-post. We can buy all we want when we get there. You've helped me out of my scrape."

"Seems to me it was easy enough to think of that."

It may have been, but Murray felt very grateful to Steve. The latter now put down his magazine and went to the door in his turn, for he, too, had a large amount of thinking to do.

William O. Stoddard

"Murray, they are taking down the lodges again."

"Going forward to-night, eh? I'm glad of that. I must spur old Many Bears up to it. Don't want him to lose a day on the road."

"Nor I either. They'll move slowly enough anyhow."

"Oh, they'll find a good place to leave the village, while the chiefs and warriors go on to be present at the treaty talk."

"Suppose there isn't any?"

"There's pretty sure to be something of the kind at this season of the year. Anyhow, we will get them to the right place for us to buy our ponies and blankets, and we will have Rita with us."

It was pretty hard, and he felt it in every corner of his heart, that he could not send for her at once and tell her all about his plans for her release. Yes, and about the beautiful home to which he meant to take her, away beyond the great salt sea she had never seen.

CHAPTER XXIX

Captain Skinner and his miners were well mounted, and they were tough, seasoned horsemen. They were in a great hurry, too, for their minds were full of dreams of the grand good times they meant to have. Some of them talked and laughed and even sung over their plans for the future. Others, older or of more quiet disposition, rode forward in good-humored silence all the many long miles of that second day.

The only thing to be done, now they were once for all beyond the reach of enemies, was to get to a place where they could exchange their gold-dust and nuggets and ingots for coin, and then spend that.

Captain Skinner had been compelled to hear nearly all of them say, one after another, and in very much the same way,

"It's a great pity, Cap, we didn't get out them twenty-dollar pieces, and leave bullion instead."

He had only replied two or three times,

"No use, boys. All under the false bottom, at the hind end of the wagon. No time to go for 'em. Had to take what was handiest."

They made an astonishingly long day's march, and did not meet with the slightest sign of danger. Nor did they come across any better token of civilized life than two deserted "ranches," or farm-houses, made of "abode" or sunburnt brick.

That night they slept soundly on their blankets in the open air, and perhaps some of them dreamed that in a few nights more they would have roofs over their heads, and wake up in the morning to find hot coffee on the breakfast-table. No bell rung for them, however, when breakfast time came, and they had nearly completed their simple meal of broiled beef and cold water when their ears were saluted by a very different sound from that of a bell.

"Horses! Rifles! Mount, boys!" shouted the little Captain. "That's a cavalry bugle!"

Cavalry.

They sprung for their arms, and they mounted in hot haste, but before the last man was in the saddle the music of that bugle was close upon them. It was a good bugle, with a sweet, clear voice, and it was well played by the tall German who had somehow drifted away from the Rhine-land into that gayly dressed and glittering regiment of Mexican lancers.

"No use to fight, boys, even if they were enemies. There's more'n three hundred of 'em. Regulars, too. What on earth brings 'em away up here? Can't be there's any revolution going on."

Captain Skinner was not a man to be easily puzzled, but the appearance of such a force there and then was a remarkable circumstance—altogether unaccountable. So was the action taken by the Mexican colonel in command. No message of inquiry was sent forward. No greeting was offered. The only sound to be heard was that of the bugle as it repeated the signals called for by the few brief, sternly uttered orders that rung out from the head of the column.

"It isn't too late for us to run, Cap," suggested Bill.

"Yes, it is. They'd catch us in no time. Besides, we haven't done anything to run for."

"Not to them we haven't."

In a few minutes more it was too late, if it had not been just then, for the gleaming lances of a full company of the Mexicans began to shine above the grass and bushes behind the miners.

"Trapped, boys! I wonder what they're going to do?"

The Mexican commander was nearly ready to tell them now, for, as his really splendid-looking horsemen closed steadily in upon the silent squad of wild-looking desperadoes, he himself rode forward toward them, accompanied by two officers in brilliant uniforms.

Captain Skinner rode out as if to meet him, but was greeted by an imperative, loud-voiced,

"Halt! Dismount!"

The fire flashed from the eyes of the ragged little Captain.

"Close up, boys! Dismount behind your horses, and take aim across the saddle."

He was obeyed like clock-work, and it was the colonel's turn to "halt," for no less than three of those deadly dark tubes were pointing straight at him, and he saw with what sort of men he was dealing. Had they been six dozen instead of only less than two, they would not have hesitated a second about charging in upon his gay lancers, and would probably have scattered them right and left.

"What are you doing here?" he demanded of Captain Skinner.

"Travelling."

"Where are you going?"

"Going to try and mind our own business."

"Where did you come from?"

"Across the border. Driven out of the mines by Apaches. Didn't expect to find Mexican regular cavalry worse than the redskins."

"We will see about that, senor. You are our prisoners."

"All right, so long as none of you come too near. It won't be healthy for any of you to try."

"No harm is intended you, senor. We are sent to guard this frontier against the Apaches, and to put down a small pronunciamento."

Captain Skinner knew what that meant. There had been some sort of a little revolution in that part of Mexico, and he and his men were suspected of having crossed the border to take part in it.

"All right, colonel. All we want is to march right along. We can pay our own way."

That was the first blunder the wily Captain had made.

The regiment of lancers, like a great many other Mexican regiments, was only "regular" because it happened just then to be employed by the national government. Its pay had not been regular at all, and the minds of both officers and men were excited by the mention of such a thing.

A half-scornful smile shot across the dark face of the colonel as he looked at those ragged men, and wondered how much they would be likely to pay for anything, even if they were not disposed to help themselves without paying. A young officer at his side was more sagacious, and suggested,

"I beg a thousand pardons, colonel, but they are miners."

"Ah! They may have been successful."

The expression of his face underwent a rapid change, and there was nothing scornful in it when he remarked to Captain Skinner that the price of a written "safe-conduct" for him and his men would be a hundred dollars each.

"That's reasonable, Cap."

"We won't mind that."

"Pay him. It's the best we can do."

"All right, Senor Colonel," said the Captain. "We will pay you in gold as soon as it's written."

One of the young officers at once dismounted, and produced

a supply of writing materials.

The "safe-conduct" was a curious document, and nothing exactly like it could have been had or bought of any cavalry officer in the United States. It was written in Spanish, of course, and it appeared to vouch for the peaceable and honest character and intentions of the entire company of miners.

The latter stood sternly behind their horses, in a dangerous looking circle, while the bargain was making, and the Captain himself had coin enough to pay for them all without calling for contributions.

The colonel was very polite now, and gave very accurate advice and instructions as to the route the miners would do well to follow.

Captain Skinner's second blunder was that he determined to go by the road laid out for him by the colonel.

Perhaps he might not have done so if he had read one other piece of paper that the young officer wrote for his colonel to sign. Or if he had seen it handed to a lancer, who rode away with it at full speed along the precise path the colonel was describing.

It was addressed, with many titles and formalities, to "General Vincente Garcia," and it was delivered by the lancer postman within three hours.

There was something remarkable in the quantity and quality of the politeness expressed by the Mexican officers after that money had been paid. Not only did they declare their great pleasure at meeting so distinguished a party of "caballeros," but also a great deal of regret at parting with them.

"That's all serene, Cap," said Bill, "but they'd have rid right over us if we'd ha' let 'em."

"We're all right now. Let's make a long push today."

The colonel showed no disposition to detain them, and it was not until they had been on their southward march for an hour that he wheeled his glittering column in the same direction.

Captain Skinner and his men knew nothing about that, and when noon came they found a capital camping-place, precisely as it had been described to them. A beautiful spot it was, with groves of shady trees and a fine spring of water, and there was more than one drove of long-horned cattle in sight.

"Somebody or other's careless about his critters," remarked one of the miners; but the Captain's face was sober.

"It looks too much as if they'd been driven up this way to feed the cavalry on. I don't like it."

"Cap, do you hear that? If it ain't another bugle you can shoot me!"

More than one was heard within the next half-hour, and three consecutive squadrons of lancers rode within sight of the miners' camp and dismounted for their noon-day meal.

They had a perfect right to do so. They were in their own country. Besides, they were not interfering with anybody. There was a good many of them, to be sure, and it was a curious thing that they should happen to come.

"Thar's too big a crop o' lancers this year to suit me," muttered Bill. "Thar's a squad of 'em coming now."

Not a large squad; only a couple of officers and their orderlies, on a very proper errand, very politely done.

It was their duty, they said, with many apologies. General Garcia desired to know who were his neighbors, and so forth.

The colonel's "safe-conduct" was shown them, and they actually touched their hats when they read it.

It was entirely satisfactory, they said. Perfect. The general would be glad to know that all was in due form. Would Captain Skinner do them the great favor to go with them and pay his respects to the general? Or would one of the other caballeros? The general would be glad to sign the "safe-conduct" himself, as the officer In supreme command of the district.

That was precisely what the Captain thought he wanted, and he consented at once.

"Cap," said Bill, "can't you get one of them civil-talkin' chaps to let us have some coffee? Or a side o' bacon?"

The officer understood him, and his bow and smile were of the most polished order as he replied, "Certainly, senor. We will be only too happy. But we hope to have the happiness of your presence at our own mess at dinner to-day. We can promise you something better than camp-fare."

"We are too many, senor," said Captain Skinner.

"Too many, Captain! We shall not have a caballero at each mess. Some of us will be disappointed."

He repeated his invitation, with a tempting list of the good things to be had at the regimental campfires, and the miners assented like one man. They had had no coffee for long months, nor bread, nor tobacco, nor vegetables, and the mere mention of such things entirely overcame their prudence.

They all abandoned their lunch of cold beef, mounted their horses, and followed the polite officers and Captain Skinner.

Their promised "good time" had come to them sooner than they had expected, and they were all jubilant over it.

The Mexicans were as good as their word, and the miners were astonished at the cordial hospitality of their welcome in the cavalry camp. Every "mess" came forward to claim a guest, and they were speedily distributed in a way which left no two of them together.

Captain Skinner found General Garcia as polite as any of the others. Not a word would he speak about business until after dinner, and so the Captain did not know till then how great a mistake he had made in permitting his men to be scattered.

"You will permit us to go on with our journey, of course, will you not, general?" said he at last, over his coffee.

"Certainly. Without doubt. We shall not detain you an hour. But the senor is a caballero of experience and knowledge. He will understand that I cannot permit so strong a body of foreigners to march through my district armed?"

"Armed? We always go armed."

"At home. Of course. You have your own laws and customs. I must enforce those of Mexico, and this district is under martial law."

William O. Stoddard

So smiling and so polite was the general, that Captain Skinner could almost believe he was sorry to be compelled to enforce that law.

He tried, therefore, to argue the point, and was still trying when one of his men came rushing up, knocking over a Mexican as he came, and shouting, "Cap, they've took every weapon I had while I was eatin'! And they won't give them up."

"Will Senor Skinner do me the favor to tell his friend that this is by my order?" The general smiled as he said it.

It was another half-hour before the different "messes" in all parts of the camp brought up to "headquarters" each its angry and disarmed guest.

"It's no use, boys," said Captain Skinner to his crestfallen band. "It's martial law, and we may as well submit. We'd best mount and ride now."

Again General Garcia felt called upon to smile and be very polite. His command was greatly in need of horses. Those of the American caballeros were just suited to cavalry use.

"Oh, if we only had our rifles, Cap!" exclaimed Bill. "Anyhow, we'll get our saddles back."

More than one bearded face grew a little pale at the thought of those saddles. The general's own chief of staff had attended to their transfer from the backs of the splendid American horses to those of the wretched little Mexican ponies, and he had noticed how heavy they all were. It was his duty, therefore, to search them, and not a saddle among them all was now any heavier than a saddle of that size ought to be.

"The ponies," remarked the polite Mexican, "are not strong enough to carry all that gold bullion as well as those heavy Gringo miners."

It was a sad dinner-party for Captain Skinner and his miners. And it turned out as he feared, for not an ounce of stolen gold was to be found in the pockets of that ragged band within ten days of their "first dinner."

William O. Stoddard

CHAPTER XXX

The day the village was moved from the bank of the river was in many ways unsatisfactory to Ni-ha-be, and so was the next and the next. Nothing went to suit her, whether in camp or on the march.

Her father was continually having grave talks with Send Warning. Red Wolf seemed to feel that he could not even ride out after deer or buffalo unless he was accompanied by Knotted Cord. He declared that no Apache "young brave" could surpass the pale-face boy in handling the lance, and that he could even make a good use of a bow and arrows.

But all that was nothing to the remarkable conduct of Dolores. Ni-ha-be was sure Rita had never before received such a degree of attention and respect from the great cook. She had even seen her adopted sister helped to broiled venison again and again before a morsel had been handed to her, the born heiress of the great chief. Her keen black eyes put on a continual watchfulness and they soon detected other strange things, and so did her quick, suspicious ears. She saw Rita look in the face of Send Warning as if she had known him all her life, and she was sure she had heard both him and Knotted Cord speak to her in the detested tongue of their race.

It was all the work of those miserable talking leaves, and

they were therefore the worst kind of "bad medicine." She would have burnt them up if she could, but now they were no longer within her reach. Rita had one, but Send Warning and his young friend had taken possession of the others, and were "listening to them" at every opportunity.

Steve said to Murray that the reading of those magazines made him feel as if he were half-way home again.

"We're anything but that, Steve. What do you think old Many Bears proposed this morning?"

"I can't guess."

"Wants to adopt us into his band. Have us marry Indian wives, and settle down."

"Tell him I'm too young. Can't take care of a squaw."

"So I did, and he answered, 'Ugh! Buy squaw some time. No hurry. Young brave good.'"

"Tell him you don't want a wife, but you'd like to buy a daughter, and keep her for me when I get old enough."

"Steve!"

"Now, Murray, I didn't mean to offend you."

"I'm not offended. It's an idea. It's a good one. It would sound right in Indian ears. I will think about it. I've been an Indian so long I hardly know how it would sound to my friends in England."

"They wouldn't care what you did, I guess, to get Rita out of the hands of the Apaches."

"Of course they would not."

Still, it was a delicate piece of business, and Murray went at it very carefully.

That afternoon, as they were riding along side by side, Many Bears again remarked to him that he would be better off among his Apache friends than anywhere else.

"Have lodge. Have squaw. Be chief a little. Be great brave."

"Got good lodge now."

"Yes, but lodge empty. Want squaw."

"Send Warning is old. No child. Rather have daughter. He has taken the Knotted Cord for a son. All he needs now is a young squaw. Keep her for young brave by-and-by."

"Ugh! Good! All Apaches say Send Warning is wise. Know what he likes best. Buy young squaw. Braves get killed in fight. Plenty young squaw have no father. All glad to come into good lodge. Have plenty meat. Plenty nice blanket. Old warrior make 'em behave, too. Good for squaw."

The notion of Many Bears was one that fitted him very well, for as chief of the band it was his duty to keep an eye upon the fortunes of its "orphans." There could be no better "asylum" for one of them than the lodge of a wise old brave like Send Warning.

"No," said Murray, after a moment of silence. "Only one young squaw in camp for me. The great chief must let me have Rita."

Many Bears was as nearly startled as an Indian chief could

be by the sudden and daring proposal, although it was not at all the same as if Murray had spoken of Ni-ha-be. He pondered a moment, and then shook his head.

"Rita will be the squaw of a great chief. He will bring me many ponies. Heap give."

Any chief in want of a wife would expect to bring rich presents, all the richer if he were to come for the daughter of a great man like Many Bears. Something far beyond the power of a seemingly poor warrior like Send Warning.

"Good," said Murray, calmly. "Heap give. Suppose you say what you think? How big heap?"

There was a grim smile on the face of Many Bears as he turned and looked in the face of his friend. "How much? Ugh! Suppose big chief bring fifty ponies?"

"Good," said Murray. "Go on."

"Fifty new blanket?"

"Good. All right."

"Five new gun. Fifty knife. Much heap powder. Big roll cloth for squaws. What say?"

"Good. All right."

"Much pistol, too. Suppose chief think of something more?"

"All right. Send Warning give it all."

"Ugh! No got 'em. No find 'em. Send Warning laugh at chief. Bad."

There was an offended look in his eyes, but Murray laid his hand on his arm, saying,

"Listen! Send Warning is white. He is a great man among his own people. He can give heap to chief. Can't find all here. Out on plains. Up in mountains. Go to fort. See blue-coat chief. See traders. Get all he wants there."

"Ugh! Good. Make talking leaf. Send it to fort. Young brave carry it. All things come back."

Many Bears had seen something of that kind done, and had never ceased envying the white man's power to obtain presents by means of a little piece of paper. Murray replied,

"No. Send Warning in no hurry. Wait till we get to fort."

That would not be for many days; and the more Many Bears thought of all the good things he had mentioned the more anxious he became to see his adopted daughter set up in a lodge of her own. Or at least under the care of a warrior who was willing to give such a "big heap" for the privilege. He "thought of something more" almost every hour from that time on, but his demands were mainly for items of moderate cost, and he did not feel at liberty to mention any larger number of ponies or blankets.

"We can buy the blankets easily enough," said Steve, when he was told the terms of the bargain, "but what about the ponies?"

"Cheaper than blankets, my boy. I've seen droves of them going for ten dollars a head. We won't have to give more than twenty. As to the other things there are always traders around the posts."

They had already counted the contents of their little buckskin bags, and Steve had been surprised to find how much money there was in little more than twenty pounds of gold coin. He had found, indeed, a strange pleasure in counting it over and over, while Murray told him of his beautiful home away across the sea.

"You'll be a rich man there."

"Have three or four times as much as this every year. You must come and visit with me, Steve, as soon as you've seen your own people."

"I dare not think much of them, Murray. I can't talk about them. It will be time enough when I learn if any of them are yet alive."

"Your father and mother?"

"Don't, Murray. I'd rather talk about Rita and our plans here."

Poor Ni-ha-be! It was not many days after that before Mother Dolores one morning called her into the lodge.

"Ni-ha-be, Rita is going to the lodge of Send Warning!"

"She shall not! He is to old. His head is white. He is ugly. I will not let her go. He is a pale-face."

"So is she."

"She is an Apache now. She is my sister. He shall not have her."

"She is to be his daughter."

William O. Stoddard

"Ugh! Then he will take her away."

"No. He will stay with us."

"Will the Knotted Cord stay?"

"Of course. He is to be the son of Send Warning."

"Ugh! Good. He is young. He is poor. He has no ponies. He will never have any. Send Warning is poor. How will he pay for Rita?"

"He is rich among his people. He is a great chief."

Ni-ha-be sprung out of the lodge and looked hurriedly around for her adopted sister. Rita had never imagined till that moment how much she was loved by the earnest-hearted Apache girl. Ni-ha-be's arms were twining around her neck, and she was weeping bitterly as she exclaimed,

"He shall not take you away from me. You are not a pale-face any more. You are Apache!"

Rita could not help crying, for the idea of the change which was coming to her was getting more and more difficult to deal with.

They were interrupted by the stately approach of old Many Bears.

"Young squaws foolish. Know nothing. Must laugh. Go to lodge now. Three days go to fort."

Three days? Was it so near? The two friends were glad to go into the lodge, as they were told, and cry it out together.

The nearest United States post at which there were likely to be any traders was still a "two days' journey" to the northward, but Many Bears had actually now received a message from his tribe that there would be "heap presents" for those who should come in time to get them, and he was more than ever anxious to discover if Send Warning had been telling him the truth. His first proposition had been, as before, that Murray should send for what he wanted, and have it brought to the Apache camp, but that had been declared out of the question.

"Ugh! Good. Then Send Warning go with chief. Buy pony. Buy heap other things. Come back and take young squaw to lodge."

"No. The great chief can bring young squaw with him. Send Warning take then what he pay for. Give pony, take young squaw."

After some little argument this was agreed to, but there were almost as serious objections made to Steve Harrison's joining the party who were to visit the post.

"Tell them I'm going anyhow," said Steve to Red Wolf, "whether they like it or not. You come too. I'll buy you a new rifle. Best there is at the fort."

That settled the matter, but Steve did not imagine how much difficulty he would have in getting hold of a rifle for an Indian. He was at last, as it turned out, compelled to keep his word by giving Red Wolf his own, and then buying another for himself from one of the traders.

But Dolores and Ni-ha-be were to be of the party. The first because Many Bears would need to "eat great heap," and the second because she had made up her mind to it very positively and would not give the matter up.

"Rita," said Murray, in a low voice, the morning they rode out of the village-camp, "take a good look back. That's the last you will ever see of it."

Then for the first rime it came into the mind of Rita that she loved not only Ni-ha-be, but all those wild, dark, savage people among whom she had been living ever since she was a little girl. She forgot for the moment how she came among them. She only remembered that the village, with all its wandering, had been her home.

"Father, will I never see any of them again?"

"I think not, Rita."

"You will let me send them presents, will you not?"

"As many as you please, Rita."

"Then I will make the whole village happy some day."

The ride to the fort was a somewhat hurried one, for Many Bears was in some fear lest all the presents should be given out before he could come for his share, and Murray was half in dread lest he should not be able to keep his own promise to the chief.

His first difficulty was removed almost at once, on his arrival, by his finding a trader who had bought a great many more ponies than he knew what to do with. Fifty of them were promptly secured and turned over to Many Bears. Even while that was being cared for Murray sought and obtained two or three important interviews. One was with the United States Army officer in command of the post, and from him he received the promise of all the help he might need.

"Still," said the gallant major, "it will keep the Indians in better humor if you pay as you agreed."

"I mean to exactly."

"It's a little the biggest romance I ever heard of. I'll tell you what: you'd better have the final transfer made in my presence."

"Thank you heartily. That will be just the thing."

Another of Murray's calls was upon the "post barber," the next upon the traders in boots, hats, clothing etc.; and when he finished the last one, Steve Harrison, who had accompanied him, making some purchases on his own account, exclaimed,

"Why, Murray, you don't look as if you were over forty. The major won't know you, nor the chief either."

"I was almost ashamed to have my hair dyed. I did it partly for Rita's sake. So she can remember me better. Partly, I must say, so my English friends will know me."

Rita turned pale when she saw him, and did not say a word; but Ni-ha-be's face put on an expression of great disgust both for him and Steve.

"Ugh! Pale-face! Young brave better wear blanket and look like a man!"

"That's it, Ni-ha-be," said Murray. "He looks like a white man now, not like a red one."

Many Bears also took a look at Send Warning and Knotted Cord in their new rig, and it was not half an hour before he was strutting around in an old blue army uniform coat and a high-crowned hat.

The Apaches of his band declared the "talking leaves" to have told the truth; for, although there was not much of a "big talk" or treaty, there were a good many presents from their "Great Father at Washington," and they were in excellent humor.

Many Bears knew that the price to be paid for Rita was fast being got together, and he may have cared very little whether it should be called a dowry or a ransom, for he had as yet no idea but what she and her new father and Steve would go back with him to their lodge in his camp.

The romantic truth, however, had been told as a great secret to the major's wife, and she told it to the other ladies at the fort, and they all went wild together over a grand new wardrobe for Rita. Never had any daughter of the Apaches owned a tenth of the varied material the enthusiastic ladies prepared in less than twenty-four hours after they had their first glimpse of Rita.

"We must make quite an affair," said the major to Murray, "of your making the payment. Then they will not think of trying to back out."

"There would be danger to Rita, I fear, if I were to make the truth known publicly too soon."

"Of course there would. Are all your presents ready?"

"They will be to-morrow."

"Then bring them to the parade ground in the morning. I will have everything fixed for the occasion."

Major Norris was an experienced "Indian fighter," and just the man to be in command of such a post, for the reason that he had learned how much cheaper it was to have the red men as friends than as enemies. He sent word at once to Many Bears and a number of other "great chiefs" that Send Warning was also a "great chief" and that proper honor must be shown him by his pale-face friends on so great an occasion. Nothing could have better suited the pride of Many Bears, but both Dolores and Ni-ha-be bitterly resented the proposal of the white ladles to prepare Rita's toilet. They would surely have kept her to themselves if it had not been for the tact and good-sense of the major's wife, to whom Murray explained the difficulty.

"Nonsense! Tell them all the ladies of the great chief's family are invited to come to my room in the morning. Tell them it will be bad manners if they do not come."

That was enough. Ni-ha-be felt that the daughter of a great chief ought not to be impolite, and she and Dolores came with Rita in the morning. The white ladies preserved their gravity, but they all said afterward that it was great fun.

Somehow or other, Rita seemed to know the uses of her new wardrobe very well, except that hooks-and-eyes were a sort of mystery, and she had no skill in the handling of pins. Dolores was made happy by the presentation of a wonderful scarf of brilliant colors, and Ni-ha-be consented to "try on" everything that was put before her.

That was as far as they could persuade her to go, however, for she took off bonnet and dress, stockings and shoes, resuming her own pretty and neatly fitting garments. All she would keep on was a pair of bracelets sent to her by Knotted Cord. They were hardly ready when they heard the band begin to play on the parade-ground, and word came from the major to hurry.

It was quite a procession that marched out of the fort barracks with Rita, and the Apache warriors and squaws who were looking on felt that a high compliment was paid to their nation. There were the troops drawn up in splendid array, with flags, and cannon, and music, and the "white chiefs" in their bright uniforms.

There were the great warriors of several "bands" of the Apaches in their paint and feathers. There were the beautiful white squaws in their strange dresses. Many Bears had been looking very intently at a collection of things just in front of where Major Norris was standing, with Murray and Steve Harrison. Ponies, blankets, guns, all, and more than all, that had been agreed upon. No chief who was looking on could say he had ever received more than that for one of his daughters, and the heart of Many Bears swelled proudly within him. There was a cloud upon his haughty face, however, and another on that of Red Wolf, who was standing at his side.

The clouds did not disperse when they searched the approaching party of ladies with their eyes for Rita. Rita! Could that be the adopted daughter of Many Bears walking there behind Mrs. Norris and Mother Dolores? The beautiful young lady whose face was so very pale, and who was dressed so splendidly? They had never before seen her look anything like that. The band played, the soldiers "presented arms," the officers touched their hats, and Murray stepped forward and held out his right hand to Many Bears, pointing with his left to the ponies and things.

"There they are. Send Warning has kept his word. Rita is mine."

"Ugh! Good. Presents all right. Young squaw is the daughter of Send Warning."

He shook hands heartily as he said it; but Many Bears had something more on his mind, and was about to open his mouth, only waiting for the music to stop. He was farther prevented by a sign to his father and a word in Apache from Red Wolf.

"Listen!" exclaimed Many Bears. "Send Warning see ponies? See all presents?"

"Yes, I see them."

"All mine now. Give all to Red Wolf. Young brave want Rita. Give all ponies for her. All presents. All except gun. Great chief keep them. What does Send Warning say?"

"Not want pony. Not want anything. Want daughter. Keep her."

"Red Wolf is young. Come again by-and-by. Bring more pony."

"Listen," said Murray, in his turn. "I tell you a big truth. Rita is my own daughter. When you burn ranch in Mexico, many summers ago, burn mine, take horses, cattle, mules, take away little girl, all that was mine. Got little girl back now. Apaches all good friends of mine."

"Send Warning not come back to lodge?"

"Not now. Go to my own people for a while. Show them my

William O. Stoddard

daughter. Say found her again."

"Ugh! Send Warning is a wise man. Cunning chief. Throw dust in the eyes of the Apaches."

It was plain that the chief was troubled in his mind. He hardly knew whether to be angry or not, but there was no reasonable objection to Murray's doing as he pleased with his own daughter, after she had cost him so many ponies.

Murray spoke again.

"Send Warning say what great chief do. Let Ni-ha-be come with Rita to pale-face lodges. Stay awhile. Learn to hear talking leaves. Then come back to her friends. What say?"

The chief pondered a moment, but Ni-ha-be had heard and understood, and a scared look arose in her face.

"Rita! Rita! You are going away? You will not be an Apache girl any more?"

"Oh, Ni-ha-be, come with me!"

Their arms were around each other, and they were both weeping, but Ni-ha-be's mind was made up instantly.

"No. You are born white. You will go with your father. I am an Apache, and I will go with my father."

Many Bears was listening.

"Send Warning hear what young squaw say? All Apaches say good. She will stay with her own people."

Ni-ha-be consented, nevertheless, to remain with Rita at the post head-quarters as long as her friends were camped close by.

Murray and Steve were anxious to begin their return to civilization, but it would be several days before a "train" would go with an escort, and they did not care to run any farther risks.

So the "farewell" was spread over sufficient time to make all sorts of explanations and promises, and Rita's mind became so full of dreams of her new life that she could easily give up the old one.

Ni-ha-be had never seen so much of the pale-faces before, and Rita tried again and again to persuade her to change her mind, but, on the very last morning of all, she resolutely responded,

"No, Rita, you are all pale-face. All over. Head and heart both belong with white friends. Feel happy. Ni-ha-be only little Indian girl here. Out there, on plains, among mountains, Ni-ha-be is the daughter of a great chief. She is an Apache."

No doubt she was right, but she and Rita had a good long cry over it then, and probably more than one afterward. As for Dolores, she came to the fort to say good-bye, but neither Many Bears nor Red Wolf came with her.

"The heart of the great chief is sore," she said, "and he mourns for his pale-face daughter. Not want to speak."

Rita sent many kindly messages, even to Red Wolf, glad as she was that he had failed to make a bargain for her.

Out from the gates of the fort that morning wheeled the cavalry escort of the waiting "train" of supply wagons and

William O. Stoddard

traders' "outfits," and behind the cavalry rode a little group of three. The ladies of the garrison, with the major and the rest, had said their last farewells at the gates, and the homeward journey had begun.

"Steve," said Murray, "are you a Lipan or an Apache today?"

"Seems to me that is all ever so long ago. I am white again."

"So am I. At one time I had little hope that I ever should be. I never would if I had not found Rita. Oh, my daughter!"

"Father! Father, see—there she is! Oh, Ni-ha-be!"

A swift and beautiful mustang was bounding toward them across the plain from a sort of cloud of wild-looking figures at a little distance, and on its back was a form they all knew well. Nearer it came and nearer.

"She wants to say good-bye again."

Nearer still, so near that they could almost look into her dark, streaming eyes, and Rita held out her arms beseechingly; but at that moment the mustang was suddenly reined in and wheeled to the right-about, while Ni-ha-be clasped both hands upon her face.

"Ni-ha-be! Oh, Ni-ha-be!"

But she was gone like the wind, and did not come again.

"There, Rita," said her father. "It is all for the best. All your Indian life is gone, like mine and Steve's. We have something better before us now."

Choose from Thousands of 1stWorldLibrary Classics By

A. M. Barnard
Ada Leverson
Adolphus William Ward
Aesop
Agatha Christie
Alexander Aaronsohn
Alexander Kielland
Alexandre Dumas
Alfred Gatty
Alfred Ollivant
Alice Duer Miller
Alice Turner Curtis
Alice Dunbar
Allen Chapman
Alleyne Ireland
Ambrose Bierce
Amelia E. Barr
Amory H. Bradford
Andrew Lang
Andrew McFarland Davis
Andy Adams
Angela Brazil
Anna Alice Chapin
Anna Sewell
Annie Besant
Annie Hamilton Donnell
Annie Payson Call
Annie Roe Carr
Annonaymous
Anton Chekhov
Archibald Lee Fletcher
Arnold Bennett
Arthur C. Benson
Arthur Conan Doyle
Arthur M. Winfield
Arthur Ransome
Arthur Schnitzler
Arthur Train
Atticus
B.H. Baden-Powell
B. M. Bower
B. C. Chatterjee
Baroness Emmuska Orczy
Baroness Orczy
Basil King
Bayard Taylor
Ben Macomber
Bertha Muzzy Bower
Bjornstjerne Bjornson

Booth Tarkington
Boyd Cable
Bram Stoker
C. Collodi
C. E. Orr
C. M. Ingleby
Carolyn Wells
Catherine Parr Traill
Charles A. Eastman
Charles Amory Beach
Charles Dickens
Charles Dudley Warner
Charles Farrar Browne
Charles Ives
Charles Kingsley
Charles Klein
Charles Hanson Towne
Charles Lathrop Pack
Charles Romyn Dake
Charles Whibley
Charles Willing Beale
Charlotte M. Braeme
Charlotte M. Yonge
Charlotte Perkins Stetson
Clair W. Hayes
Clarence Day Jr.
Clarence E. Mulford
Clemence Housman
Confucius
Coningsby Dawson
Cornelis DeWitt Wilcox
Cyril Burleigh
D. H. Lawrence
Daniel Defoe
David Garnett
Dinah Craik
Don Carlos Janes
Donald Keyhoe
Dorothy Kilner
Dougan Clark
Douglas Fairbanks
E. Nesbit
E. P. Roe
E. Phillips Oppenheim
E. S. Brooks
Earl Barnes
Edgar Rice Burroughs
Edith Van Dyne
Edith Wharton

Edward Everett Hale
Edward J. O'Biren
Edward S. Ellis
Edwin L. Arnold
Eleanor Atkins
Eleanor Hallowell Abbott
Eliot Gregory
Elizabeth Gaskell
Elizabeth McCracken
Elizabeth Von Arnim
Ellem Key
Emerson Hough
Emilie F. Carlen
Emily Bronte
Emily Dickinson
Enid Bagnold
Enilor Macartney Lane
Erasmus W. Jones
Ernie Howard Pie
Ethel May Dell
Ethel Turner
Ethel Watts Mumford
Eugene Sue
Eugenie Foa
Eugene Wood
Eustace Hale Ball
Evelyn Everett-green
Everard Cotes
F. H. Cheley
F. J. Cross
F. Marion Crawford
Fannie E. Newberry
Federick Austin Ogg
Ferdinand Ossendowski
Fergus Hume
Florence A. Kilpatrick
Fremont B. Deering
Francis Bacon
Francis Darwin
Frances Hodgson Burnett
Frances Parkinson Keyes
Frank Gee Patchin
Frank Harris
Frank Jewett Mather
Frank L. Packard
Frank V. Webster
Frederic Stewart Isham
Frederick Trevor Hill
Frederick Winslow Taylor

Friedrich Kerst
Friedrich Nietzsche
Fyodor Dostoyevsky
G.A. Henty
G.K. Chesterton
Gabrielle E. Jackson
Garrett P. Serviss
Gaston Leroux
George A. Warren
George Ade
Geroge Bernard Shaw
George Cary Eggleston
George Durston
George Ebers
George Eliot
George Gissing
George MacDonald
George Meredith
George Orwell
George Sylvester Viereck
George Tucker
George W. Cable
George Wharton James
Gertrude Atherton
Gordon Casserly
Grace E. King
Grace Gallatin
Grace Greenwood
Grant Allen
Guillermo A. Sherwell
Gulielma Zollinger
Gustav Flaubert
H. A. Cody
H. B. Irving
H.C. Bailey
H. G. Wells
H. H. Munro
H. Irving Hancock
H. R. Naylor
H. Rider Haggard
H. W. C. Davis
Haldeman Julius
Hall Caine
Hamilton Wright Mabie
Hans Christian Andersen
Harold Avery
Harold McGrath
Harriet Beecher Stowe
Harry Castlemon
Harry Coghill
Harry Houidini

Hayden Carruth
Helent Hunt Jackson
Helen Nicolay
Hendrik Conscience
Hendy David Thoreau
Henri Barbusse
Henrik Ibsen
Henry Adams
Henry Ford
Henry Frost
Henry James
Henry Jones Ford
Henry Seton Merriman
Henry W Longfellow
Herbert A. Giles
Herbert Carter
Herbert N. Casson
Herman Hesse
Hildegard G. Frey
Homer
Honore De Balzac
Horace B. Day
Horace Walpole
Horatio Alger Jr.
Howard Pyle
Howard R. Garis
Hugh Lofting
Hugh Walpole
Humphry Ward
Ian Maclaren
Inez Haynes Gillmore
Irving Bacheller
Isabel Cecilia Williams
Isabel Hornibrook
Israel Abrahams
Ivan Turgenev
J.G.Austin
J. Henri Fabre
J. M. Barrie
J. M. Walsh
J. Macdonald Oxley
J. R. Miller
J. S. Fletcher
J. S. Knowles
J. Storer Clouston
J. W. Duffield
Jack London
Jacob Abbott
James Allen
James Andrews
James Baldwin

James Branch Cabell
James DeMille
James Joyce
James Lane Allen
James Lane Allen
James Oliver Curwood
James Oppenheim
James Otis
James R. Driscoll
Jane Abbott
Jane Austen
Jane L. Stewart
Janet Aldridge
Jens Peter Jacobsen
Jerome K. Jerome
Jessie Graham Flower
John Buchan
John Burroughs
John Cournos
John F. Kennedy
John Gay
John Glasworthy
John Habberton
John Joy Bell
John Kendrick Bangs
John Milton
John Philip Sousa
John Taintor Foote
Jonas Lauritz Idemil Lie
Jonathan Swift
Joseph A. Altsheler
Joseph Carey
Joseph Conrad
Joseph E. Badger Jr
Joseph Hergesheimer
Joseph Jacobs
Jules Vernes
Julian Hawthrone
Julie A Lippmann
Justin Huntly McCarthy
Kakuzo Okakura
Karle Wilson Baker
Kate Chopin
Kenneth Grahame
Kenneth McGaffey
Kate Langley Bosher
Kate Langley Bosher
Katherine Cecil Thurston
Katherine Stokes
L. A. Abbot
L. T. Meade

L. Frank Baum
Latta Griswold
Laura Dent Crane
Laura Lee Hope
Laurence Housman
Lawrence Beasley
Leo Tolstoy
Leonid Andreyev
Lewis Carroll
Lewis Sperry Chafer
Lilian Bell
Lloyd Osbourne
Louis Hughes
Louis Joseph Vance
Louis Tracy
Louisa May Alcott
Lucy Fitch Perkins
Lucy Maud Montgomery
Luther Benson
Lydia Miller Middleton
Lyndon Orr
M. Corvus
M. H. Adams
Margaret E. Sangster
Margret Howth
Margaret Vandercook
Margaret W. Hungerford
Margret Penrose
Maria Edgeworth
Maria Thompson Daviess
Mariano Azuela
Marion Polk Angellotti
Mark Overton
Mark Twain
Mary Austin
Mary Catherine Crowley
Mary Cole
Mary Hastings Bradley
Mary Roberts Rinehart
Mary Rowlandson
M. Wollstonecraft Shelley
Maud Lindsay
Max Beerbohm
Myra Kelly
Nathaniel Hawthrone
Nicolo Machiavelli
O. F. Walton
Oscar Wilde

Owen Johnson
P.G. Wodehouse
Paul and Mabel Thorne
Paul G. Tomlinson
Paul Severing
Percy Brebner
Percy Keese Fitzhugh
Peter B. Kyne
Plato
Quincy Allen
R. Derby Holmes
R. L. Stevenson
R. S. Ball
Rabindranath Tagore
Rahul Alvares
Ralph Bonehill
Ralph Henry Barbour
Ralph Victor
Ralph Waldo Emmerson
Rene Descartes
Ray Cummings
Rex Beach
Rex E. Beach
Richard Harding Davis
Richard Jefferies
Richard Le Gallienne
Robert Barr
Robert Frost
Robert Gordon Anderson
Robert L. Drake
Robert Lansing
Robert Lynd
Robert Michael Ballantyne
Robert W. Chambers
Rosa Nouchette Carey
Rudyard Kipling
Saint Augustine
Samuel B. Allison
Samuel Hopkins Adams
Sarah Bernhardt
Sarah C. Hallowell
Selma Lagerlof
Sherwood Anderson
Sigmund Freud
Standish O'Grady
Stanley Weyman
Stella Benson
Stella M. Francis

Stephen Crane
Stewart Edward White
Stijn Streuvels
Swami Abhedananda
Swami Parmananda
T. S. Ackland
T. S. Arthur
The Princess Der Ling
Thomas A. Janvier
Thomas A Kempis
Thomas Anderton
Thomas Bailey Aldrich
Thomas Bulfinch
Thomas De Quincey
Thomas Dixon
Thomas H. Huxley
Thomas Hardy
Thomas More
Thornton W. Burgess
U. S. Grant
Upton Sinclair
Valentine Williams
Various Authors
Vaughan Kester
Victor Appleton
Victor G. Durham
Victoria Cross
Virginia Woolf
Wadsworth Camp
Walter Camp
Walter Scott
Washington Irving
Wilbur Lawton
Wilkie Collins
Willa Cather
Willard F. Baker
William Dean Howells
William le Queux
W. Makepeace Thackeray
William W. Walter
William Shakespeare
Winston Churchill
Yei Theodora Ozaki
Yogi Ramacharaka
Young E. Allison
Zane Grey